RED RAVEN

PART 107 GUIDEBOOK

A COMPLETE STUDY GUIDE FOR THE FAA PART 107 REMOTE PILOT CERTIFICATION

Version 1.0 | September 2025

By Michael Wilson and Derrick Ward

RED RAVEN

UAS TRAINING & PROGRAM DEVELOPMENT

Published by Red Raven UAS
Los Angeles, California

www.redravenuas.com

Version 1.0 | September 2025

Publisher: Red Raven UAS
Los Angeles, California
www.redravenuas.com

ISBN: [979-8-9931892-0-8]

Printed in the United States of America

Disclaimer

This guide is an independent publication and is not affiliated with, endorsed by, or sponsored by the Federal Aviation Administration (FAA).

This guide is designed to provide information and educational material to help prepare an applicant for the Federal Aviation Administration (FAA) Part 107 Aeronautical Knowledge Test. The authors and publisher have made every effort to ensure the accuracy and completeness of the information contained in this book as of the date of publication. However, aviation regulations, procedures, and test standards are subject to change. The reader is solely responsible for consulting official FAA sources and complying with the most current regulations.

This book is sold with the understanding that the publisher and authors are not engaged in rendering legal, professional, or official flight instruction services. The ultimate responsibility for the safe and legal operation of any unmanned aircraft rests entirely with the Remote Pilot in Command (RPIC). The publisher and authors shall not be held liable for any damages, losses, or legal actions resulting from the use of or reliance on the information provided in this guide. Passing the knowledge test is not guaranteed and depends on the individual's study and preparation. Nothing in this guide constitutes legal advice.

For our families and friends, whose support gives us wings.

And for those who dare to fly — may this book be your lift-off.

Contents

Welcome, future drone pilot!

So, you're ready to take to the skies and join the exciting world of unmanned aviation Awesome! At Red Raven, we're excited to be your wingmen on this adventure.

When we first looked at what's out there for aspiring drone pilots to pass the FAA's Part 107 Exam, we found most of it to be complicated, confusing, and—let's be real—about as thrilling as reading a toaster manual.

Flying should be fun, not a chore. That's why we built this guide: to make the journey exciting, clear, and just challenging enough to keep you sharp.

We designed this guide to be:

- **Easy to read:** No government jargon, just plain English.

- **Engaging:** A little personality to keep you from falling asleep.

- **Comprehensive:** Everything you need to pass, all in one place.

We've taken decades of combined drone-industry experience – from real-world flying to problem-solving in the field – and distilled it into the ultimate no-nonsense guide. Inside, you'll find exactly what matters, why it matters, and what you need to know to ace the FAA Part 107 exam and become a certified remote pilot.

Congratulations on taking the first step. We're honored to be part of your journey to earning your Remote Pilot Certificate. Let's go get it!

Michael Wilson & Derrick Ward
Founders, Red Raven UAS

Introduction

Welcome to the World of Drones!

So, you've got your hands on a drone (or not yet), and you're ready to see the world from a whole new perspective. We get it! The thrill of piloting your own aircraft, capturing breathtaking aerial views, and exploring the endless possibilities of drone technology is what gets us excited at Red Raven too. But before you can launch your drone for commercial purposes, there's a small hurdle to clear: the FAA Part 107 Exam.

Don't worry, it's not as scary as it sounds! This exam ensures that you have the knowledge and skills to operate your drone safely and responsibly, sharing the skies with other aircraft.

Decoding the FAA's Lingo

Let's start by decoding the basics:

- **What is "Part 107"?** The rules for drone pilots are found in Title 14 of the Code of Federal Regulations (CFR). "Part 107" is simply the specific section of that code that deals with Small Unmanned Aircraft Systems.

- **What is the test called?** The official name for the exam you will take to receive your remote pilot certificate is the "Unmanned Aircraft General – Small (UAG)" knowledge test.

- **What is the drone license called?** After you pass the test, you will be issued a "Remote Pilot Certificate with a small UAS rating." That is your official "license to fly".

What to Expect on Your Journey

Your journey to becoming a licensed drone pilot will be a mix of learning, practice, and a little bit of studying. Here's a sneak peek of what's ahead:

- **Learning the Rules of the Sky:** Just like driving a car, flying a drone has its own set of rules. We'll guide you through the essential FAA regulations in a way that's easy to understand and remember.

- **Becoming a Weather Watcher:** You'll learn how to read weather reports and understand how wind, rain, and even the sun can affect your drone's performance.

- **Mastering the Art of Flight Planning:** From choosing your flight path to calculating your drone's weight and balance, you'll learn how to plan every flight like a pro.

- **Thinking Like a Pilot:** We'll help you develop the critical thinking skills you need to make smart decisions and handle any unexpected situations that may come your way.

So, let's get started on this exciting journey together. By the time you finish this guide, you'll be more than ready to ace your exam and take your passion for drones to new heights!

Why This Guidebook Exists

The FAA has created their own handbook called the *Remote Pilot – Small Unmanned Aircraft Systems Study Guide* on everything you need to know to pass the Part 107 Exam and become a certified drone pilot. But the FAA has a tendency to overly complicate things. For instance, in their official guide, they list 17 different publications as your primary study references shown in **Figure 0.1**.

Reference	Title
14 CFR part 47	Aircraft Registration
14 CFR part 48	Registration and Marking Requirements for Small Unmanned Aircraft Systems
14 CFR part 71	Designation of Class A, B, C, D and E Airspace Areas; Air Traffic Service Rotes; and Reporting Points
14 CFR part 107	Operation and Certification of Small Unmanned Aircraft Systems
AC 00-6	Aviation Weather for Pilots and Flight Operations Personnel
AC 150/5200-32	Reporting Wildlife Aircraft Strikes
AC 107-2	Small Unmanned Aircraft Systems (sUAS)
AIM	Aeronautical Information Manual
FAA-CT-8080-2	Airman Knowledge Testing Supplement for Sport Pilot, Recreational Pilot, and Private Pilot
FAA-G-8082-20	Remote Pilot Knowledge Test Guide
FAA-H-8083-1	Weight & Balance Handbook
FAA-H-8083-2	Risk Management Handbook
FAA-H-8083-25	Pilot's Handbook of Aeronautical Knowledge
FAA-S-ACS-10	Remote Pilot – Small Unmanned Aircraft Systems Airman Certification Standards
SAFO 09013	Fighting Fires Caused By Lithium Type Batteries in Portable Electronic Devices
SAFO 10015	Flying in the wire environment
SAFO 10017	Risks in Transporting Lithium Batteries in Cargo by Aircraft
SAFO 15010	Carriage of Spare Lithium Batteries in Carry-on and Checked Baggage

Figure 0.1. FAA Study References. (Source: FAA-G-8082-22, pg. 74)

You read that right. That's the 6,000-page mountain of technical jargon the FAA expects you to climb. To put that in perspective, the flight manual for the Saturn V rocket—the one that put a man on the moon—was barely 250 pages long. You're not trying to go to the moon here—You just want to fly a drone.

The worst part is, they ask you to consistently reference them for more information and images. They want you to read their guidebook while flipping back and forth between this headache-inducing pile of documents? That doesn't seem right. Expecting a new pilot to read all their official study materials is like asking someone to read the entire dictionary from cover to cover before they're allowed to read Harry Potter.

Why is this all so complicated?

As anyone who's ever looked at the U.S. tax code knows, the government doesn't always do simple, and that's why we're here—to cut through the bureaucratic language and give you the straight talk.

We've done the hard work of digging through this dumpster fire and taking out just the things that are worth saving to your brain. We'll give you just enough information to:

1. **Fly your drone safely.**

2. **Comply with all the rules.**

3. **Ace the questions on the official exam.**

4. **Simplify the convoluted process of getting your license to fly.**

The best part is, the Red Raven Guide has everything you need. You will never have to look at another book, guide, or document to get your pilot's certificate.

Here's how we've boiled down our method of teaching versus the FAA's.

FAA vs. Red Raven – Study Experience

CATEGORY	FAA WAY	RED RAVEN WAY
Study Material	17 publications, nearly 6,000 pages of dense technical language	1 streamlined guide, everything you need in plain English
Reading Level	Lawyer + rocket scientist	Regular human
Focus	Covers everything, whether it's on the test or not	Covers what's on the test + what actually helps you fly
Learning Style	Long paragraphs, outdated diagrams, and FAA jargon	Clear explanations and real-world examples
Time Commitment	Weeks (and that's if you're a speed reader)	Days–learning at your own pace
Motivation Factor	Risk of boredom-induced coma	Keeps you engaged and confident
End Result	Confused, over-prepared in the wrong areas	Prepared for the test and real-world flying

Table 0.1

So What's Next?

By now you're starting to see the FAA's playbook: a world of technical jargon, endless documents, and enough acronyms to make your head spin. But here's the deal: you don't have to read the dictionary just to get to the magic. We've already flipped through all 6,000 pages of government-speak and we've compiled it into this guide. All killer, no filler.

We've made it our mission to make sure you're prepared for both the test and the real world. Are there some things in this guide we personally wouldn't bother teaching you if we were just training you to be a good remote pilot? Yes. Why are they in here? Because they are on the test. Is it good knowledge to have? Yes. Will you ever use it in the field? Maybe. But here's the good news: we've boiled it down, cut out the noise, and lined up exactly what you need to focus on.

So, let's get to the good stuff. Power up your brain. Your training starts now.

The Rulebook of the Skies

Understanding FAA Regulations

Alright, let's talk about the rules. I know, I know, rules can be a drag, but trust me, these are important. Think of them as the "rules of the road" for the sky. Just like you wouldn't drive a car without knowing what a stop sign means, you don't want to fly a drone without understanding the basic regulations. This chapter will break down some of the key rules from the FAA's 14 CFR Part 107 to get you started.

The "Must-Knows" of Part 107

These are some of the essentials you need to know:

- **You're the Remote Pilot in Command (RPIC):** As the licensed drone pilot, you are the one in charge. You are responsible for the safety of the flight, and your decisions are final. It's a big responsibility, but a rewarding one!

- **Register Your Drone:** Before any commercial flight, your drone must be registered with the FAA. Any drone weighing more than 0.55 pounds (250g) must be registered via the FAA DroneZone website. Once you get your registration number, it must be clearly displayed on the exterior of your drone. Think of it as your drone's license plate —it's a non-negotiable step.

- **Keep it Under 55 lbs:** Your drone, including everything it's carrying, must weigh less than 55 pounds. That's the weight of a small- to medium-sized dog, so most consumer and professional drones will be well under this limit.

- **Fly Within Visual Line-of-Sight (VLOS):** You must always be able to see your drone with your own eyes, without binoculars or other visual aids. If you're flying with FPV goggles, you are required to have a Visual Observer (VO) who maintains VLOS on your behalf. You must stay in direct communication with the VO at all times. Even with a VO, you remain the Remote Pilot in Command (RPIC) and are fully responsible for the safe operation of the aircraft.

- **3 Miles of Visibility:** You must be able to see for 3 miles in all directions in order to fly. We'll talk about how to figure this out when we talk about weather later on.

- **Stay Below 400 Feet:** Your drone needs to stay at or below 400 feet above the ground, unless you're flying within 400 feet of a structure, like a tall building or a cell tower. In that case, you can fly up to 400 feet above the top of that structure. This helps keep drone activity away from manned aircraft.

- **Night Operations:** Under Part 107, you may fly at night provided your aircraft is equipped with anti-collision lights that are visible for at least 3 statute miles. These lights must be turned on during all night flights as well as during civil twilight (the 30 minutes before official sunrise and the 30 minutes after official sunset).

- **Stay away from clouds:** You must stay 500ft below and 2000ft horizontally away from clouds.

- **Mind Your Speed:** The maximum speed for your drone is 100 mph (or 87 knots). Most drones won't even come close to this, but it's a good number to keep in mind.

- **No Flying Over People:** You can't fly your drone over people who aren't directly participating in the operation, under a covered structure, or inside a stationary vehicle. There are some exceptions to this rule for certain categories of drones. A drone can be operated over people if it is in one of these four categories:

  - **Category 1:** The drone must weigh **less than 0.55 pounds** (250 grams) at takeoff, including everything it's carrying. It also must not contain any exposed rotating parts that could lacerate human skin. Most mini-drones (like the DJI Mini series) fall into this category.

  - **Category 2:** For drones weighing more than 0.55 pounds (250 grams), this category requires that the drone will not cause injury to a person greater than the impact of **11 foot-pounds of kinetic energy**. It also must not have any exposed rotating parts that could cut skin. Drones in this category must have a label from the manufacturer certifying that they are Category 2 compliant.

- **Category 3:** This category is for slightly heavier drones. It uses a higher injury threshold of **25 foot-pounds of kinetic energy**. The key difference is that operations in this category are limited. You cannot fly over open-air assemblies of people, and you can only fly over people if they are inside a stationary vehicle or under a protective cover (like a bus stop awning).

- **Category 4:** This is the highest level and requires the drone to have an **airworthiness certificate** from the FAA. These are typically larger, more sophisticated drones that have undergone a rigorous safety and inspection process, similar to manned aircraft.

What Does a Category 2 or 3 Drone Look Like in the Real World?

While parachutes are a very common solution, manufacturers can use several methods to ensure a drone meets the kinetic energy and no-laceration requirements for Category 2 or 3.

- **Parachute Systems:** This is a popular method. A parachute dramatically slows the drone's descent in an emergency, ensuring it impacts the ground with low kinetic energy.

- **Frangible or Breakaway Parts:** The drone could be designed with propellers or other components that are meant to break apart or shatter on impact, absorbing energy so that the main body of the drone has a softer impact.

- **Caged or Enclosed Designs:** Some drones have enclosed propellers or are built with lightweight, energy-absorbing materials that prevent lacerations and soften any impact by design.

- **No Flying From a Moving Vehicle:** You can't operate your drone from a moving vehicle, unless you're in a sparsely populated area.

- **Give Way to Manned Aircraft:** This is a non-negotiable rule. Drones must always yield the right-of-way to manned aircraft (airplanes, helicopters, etc.). If you see one, get out of the way! Believe me, you don't want to be that guy! (Or gal)

- **Pre-Flight Check is a Must:** Before every flight, you need to do a pre-flight inspection of your drone to make sure everything is in working order. We'll go over what to check for in a later chapter.

A Note on Waivers

What if you need to operate outside the standard rules? For that, you need a **waiver** from the FAA. You must apply for a waiver through the **FAA DroneZone** website by submitting a detailed safety case that proves you can conduct the operation safely.

Commonly waived rules include:

- Flying at night without the standard lighting.

- Flying beyond visual line-of-sight.

- Operating over people in ways that don't meet the four categories.

- Operating multiple sUAS

The FAA will **not** waive the rules against careless or reckless operations, the requirement for a Remote Pilot Certificate, or the 55 lb weight limit. Waivers require a written application with a strong safety case.

Remote ID

Remote ID is the FAA's "digital license plate" system for drones. It allows authorities, air traffic managers, and the public to identify and locate a drone in real time by receiving broadcast data while it's in flight.

What Remote ID broadcasts:

1. Drone identification (serial number or session ID).

2. Drone's current location, altitude, velocity, and timestamp.

3. Location of the control station (where the pilot is operating from).

4. Takeoff location.

5. Emergency status (if activated).

The goal of Remote ID is to make drone flights more transparent, deter unsafe or illegal flying, and help law enforcement quickly determine responsibility if a drone is operating in restricted areas or involved in an incident. Think of it as an electronic name tag for your drone – visible to anyone with the right receiver, even if they can't see the aircraft itself.

How to Comply with Remote ID

1. Standard Remote ID Drone (Built-In)

Most new drones from manufacturers like DJI, Autel, and Skydio already have Remote ID built in. These drones automatically broadcast the required data during flight, and this feature cannot be disabled when operating in U.S. airspace. No extra hardware is needed.

2. Remote ID Broadcast Module (Add-On Device)

For older or homebuilt drones without built-in RID, you can attach an external broadcast module. The module transmits the required identification and location data, but it uses its own ID instead of the drone's serial number. You must enter the takeoff location into the module before each flight.

3. Flying in a FRIA (FAA-Recognized Identification Area)

A FRIA is a designated flying site, such as an AMA field, RC club location, or university test range, where Remote ID is not required. Within a FRIA, you may fly drones without RID, including older or homebuilt models. However, you must remain inside the FRIA boundaries – once you leave, Remote ID compliance is required. FRIA status applies to the location, not the pilot or drone.

A Guide to Night Operations

So, you've mastered flying during the day, but you want to capture that perfect cityscape at twilight or film an event after the sun goes down. The great news is that flying at night is now easier than ever, but it comes with a new set of rules and responsibilities. This chapter will light the way.

Be Seen: Anti-Collision Lights

This is the most important piece of equipment for night flights. Your drone **must** be equipped with anti-collision lights that are visible for at least **3 statute miles**. Anti-collision lights are often called a beacon or strobe as well and are used interchangeably.

- **What kind of light?** It must be a flashing strobe light. A simple solid red or green light is not enough.

- **Can they be any color?** While the FAA doesn't specify a color, white is the industry standard as it is the most visible from a distance.

- **Do the lights that came with my drone count?** Usually, no. The standard LED lights on most drones are for your own orientation and are not bright enough to meet the 3-mile requirement. You will likely need to purchase a third-party strobe light to attach to your drone.

Most consumer drones—even some professional ones—do not come with anti-collision lights. The exceptions are usually enterprise models that are made for public safety, inspections, surveying, etc. For instance, currently the DJI Enterprise series of drones all have beacons built-in for night flying.

Seeing in the Dark

Flying at night is not the same as flying during the day. Your eyes work differently in the dark, and your ability to judge distance and movement is reduced.

Here's some tips for flying at night:

- **Scan the Sky:** You and your Visual Observer (VO) need to be even more vigilant. Spend more time looking at the dark sky around the drone rather than staring at the drone's lights. This helps you spot the faint lights of a distant airplane.

- **Know Your Area:** Before you even take off, be extra thorough in scouting your flight area for obstacles. Wires, tree branches, and poles that are easy to see during the day can become nearly invisible at night.

- **Respect the Darkness:** Your depth perception is not as good at night. Be extra cautious and fly more slowly than you normally would. Give yourself a bigger buffer from any known obstacles.

Key Takeaways

1. The four "operations over people" categories appear often on the exam.

2. Your drone needs an anti-collision strobe light visible for at least 3 statute miles.

3. Night flying requires more careful scanning of the environment and a greater awareness of potential obstacles.

4. Always remember the "big three" limits: 400 ft altitude, 100 mph speed, VLOS.

5. Remote ID is now a core requirement—expect test questions on it.

Likely Test Questions

1. What is the maximum allowed takeoff weight for a small unmanned aircraft?

2. How far before sunrise can you fly without a waiver?

3. When is flying from a moving vehicle allowed?

4. Name the four categories of operations over people.

5. What are the three ways to comply with the Remote ID requirement?

6. To operate a sUAS at night, what must the Remote Pilot in Command do?

Airspace and Sectional Charts

Sectional Charts

A sectional chart is the FAA's official "map of the sky," showing everything from airspace boundaries and airports to obstacles and terrain. Once you know how to read it, you can instantly see where you can fly, where you can't, and what authorizations you need.

Check out **Figure 2.1.** This is a sectional chart in all it's glory. Everyone remembers their first.

Overwhelming, isn't it? We know it looks like a chaotic mess of lines, colors, and symbols, and many students find it intimidating. But don't worry! We promise you by the time you get to the end of this chapter, this will start to make sense.

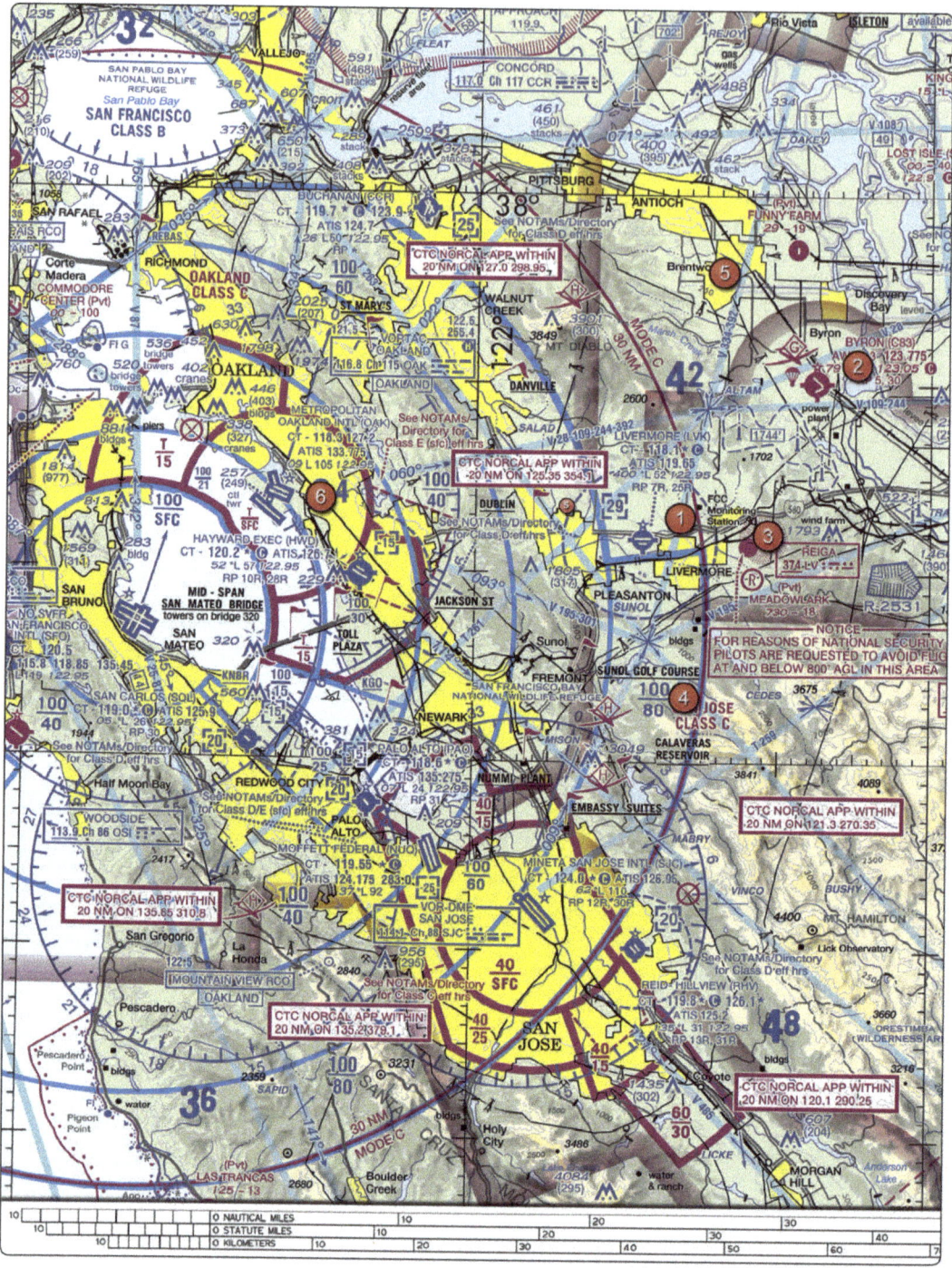

Figure 2.1. Sectional Chart Excerpt of the San Francisco Bay Area. (Source: FAA-CT-8080-2H, Figure 74)

Where do these Sectional Charts come from?

While you might not interact with these charts every day as a drone pilot, understanding them is non-negotiable—not just because it's a huge part of the exam, but because true airspace knowledge is critical for flying safely in the real world. With a little practice, you'll be able to glance at any sectional chart and know exactly what's going on.

Most of the images, charts, and diagrams you'll see in this chapter (and throughout this guide) come directly from the **FAA Airman Knowledge Testing Supplement**. This is the exact reference book you'll be given during the actual Part 107 exam. So these are all images you will see on the actual test on exam day.

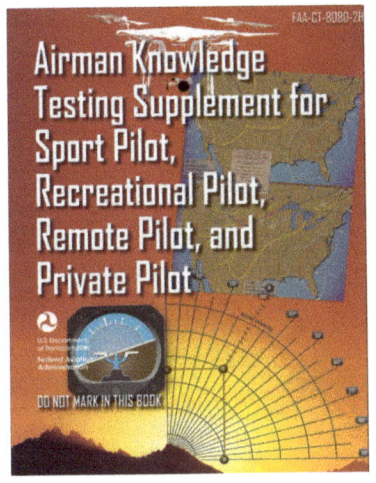

Airman Knowledge Testing Supplement

You can download the current version here:
https://www.faa.gov/sites/faa.gov/files/training_testing/testing/supplements/sport_rec_private_akts.pdf

Don't worry—you won't need to use that supplement right now. This guidebook is designed to be **standalone**, meaning all the relevant figures, charts, and examples are already included in the following pages. You'll have everything you need right here without flipping between multiple documents.

So let's move on to the first part of understanding one of these charts.

Latitude and Longitude – Finding Your Place

A sectional chart is essentially a giant grid that allows you to find the exact location of any point on Earth. This grid is made up of latitude and longitude lines shown in **Figure 2.2**.

- **Latitude (Parallels):** Think of these as the horizontal rungs of a ladder climbing up the globe. They are parallel to the Equator and measure your distance **north or south.** In the United States, you will always be dealing with North latitude.

- **Longitude (Meridians):** These are the long, vertical lines that run from the North Pole to the South Pole. They measure your distance **east or west** from the Prime Meridian in Greenwich, England. In the United States, you will always be dealing with West longitude.

Each line is marked with a number for degrees (°), and the smaller tick marks between them represent minutes ('). There are 60 minutes in a degree.

Figure 2.2. Meridians and parallels—the basis of measuring time, distance, and direction. (Source: FAA-CT-8080-2H, Figure 11-3)

Why This Matters for a Drone Pilot

While your drone's GPS handles all of this automatically, a professional pilot must know how to read and verify coordinates on a chart. You might be hired for a job where the client gives you a specific set of coordinates for the operating area, or you might need to verify the exact boundaries of a Temporary Flight Restriction (TFR). Being able to pinpoint a location on a chart is a fundamental skill of any aviator.

Let's Find an Airport

Using the chart in **Figure 2.3**, let's find the **Minot International Airport (MOT)**. Its approximate coordinates are **48°15'N, 101°17'W**. Here's how you do it:

1. **Find the Latitude Line (Horizontal):** Look near the top of the chart for the bold horizontal line labeled **48°**. This is your starting point for North-South position.

2. **Find the Longitude Line (Vertical):** Look near the center of the chart for the bold vertical line labeled **101°**. This is your starting point for East-West position.

3. **Locate the Intersection Box:** Find the box where the 48° latitude and 101° longitude lines intersect. All your work will happen inside this grid square.

4. **Pinpoint the Exact Spot:**

    *   **For Latitude (48°15'N):** Inside that box, find the small tick marks along the vertical 101° line. Each tick mark is one minute. Find the longer tick mark that represents 15 minutes and trace a line horizontally to the right.

    *   **For Longitude (101°17'W):** Now, find the tick marks along the horizontal 48° line. From the 101° line, count to the right (west) to the 17-minute mark (just past the 15-minute tick mark) and trace a line vertically upwards.

Where those two imaginary lines meet, you will see the **blue airport symbol** for Minot International (MOT).

Figure 2.3. Sectional Chart Excerpt. (Source: FAA-CT-8080-2H, Figure 21)

Airport Symbols

Now that you can find your way around the map, let's look at the most common landmarks you'll see: airports. A sectional chart like **Figure 2.4** gives you a ton of information about an airport just by the color and shape of its symbol. Knowing how to read them at a glance is a key skill.

Here are the symbols to help you identify airports:

Runway Type (The Shape of the Symbol)

  Circle with Runways: An airport with hard-surfaced runways.

 Plain Circle: An airport without hard-surfaced runways (e.g., grass or gravel).

Airport Services (The Color & Details of the Symbol)

 Blue Symbol: The airport **has** a control tower.

 Magenta Symbol: The airport is **non-towered** (no control tower).

 Star Symbol: A rotating beacon is present, used to help pilots find the airport at night.

Take a look at **Figure 2.4** and find all of the airports. You'll see they all have large circles around them.

Figure 2.4. Sectional Chart and Legend. (Source: FAA-G-8082-22, Figure 11-2)

Airspace Deciphered

The sky is a busy place, and it's divided into different "airspace classes" to keep everyone safe. Think of it like different types of roads—some are like quiet country lanes, while others are like multi-lane highways.

The FAA has a system for classifying airspace using letters of the alphabet. For drone pilots, the most important ones to know are B, C, D, E, and G. You'll rarely, if ever, encounter Class A airspace, as it starts way up at 18,000 feet.

Check out **Figure 2.5** for examples of what each airspace looks like in 3D. They look like upside down wedding cakes.

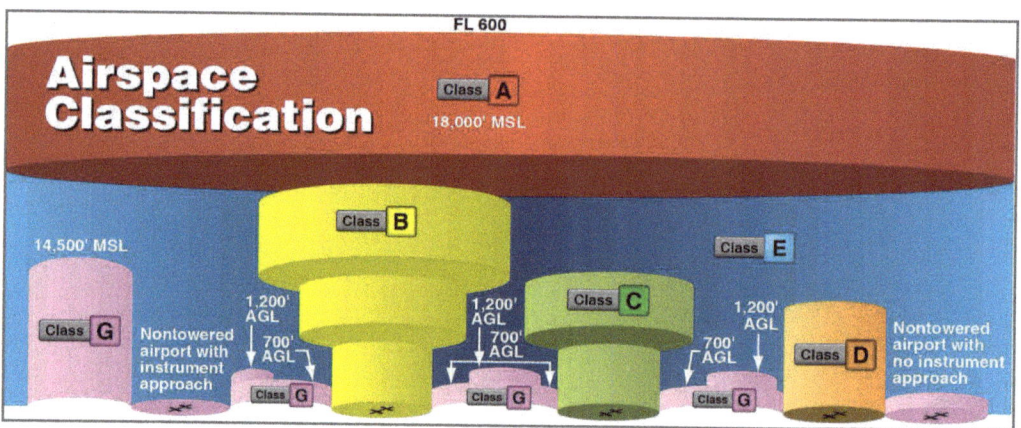

Figure 2.5. Airspace profile. (Source: FAA-G-8082-22, Figure 2-1)

Your Airspace Decoder Ring

On a sectional chart, those wedding cakes are flat in 2D, so read on so you can start seeing them pop off the map. The FAA provides a legend to explain every symbol and color.

Here's what the lines mean:

- **Class B Airspace (Solid Blue Line):** Think **B** for **Big and Busy**.
  This surrounds the nation's largest airports (e.g., LAX, ATL, ORD). Shaped like an upside-down wedding cake. Requires FAA LAANC authorization.

- **Class C Airspace (Solid Magenta Line):** Think **C** for **Congested.**
  Medium-sized airports in busy areas. Similar "cake" shape but smaller. Requires LAANC authorization.

- **Class D Airspace (Dashed Blue Line):** Think **D** for **Downtown**.
  Smaller towered airports. Simple cylinder shape. Requires LAANC authorization.

- **Class E Airspace:** The most common controlled airspace.

  - **Fuzzy Magenta Line:** Starts at 700 ft AGL; below is Class G.

  - **Fuzzy Blue Line:** Starts at 1,200 ft AGL.

  - **Dashed Magenta Line:** Starts at the **surface** for smaller airports without towers but with instrument procedures.

- **Class G Airspace (No Lines):** Think **G** for **Go for it!**
  This is uncontrolled airspace. If you're outside all colored boundaries and below the floor of Class E, you're in Class G.

A Quick Note on LAANC (Pronounced "Lance")

*You've just seen "LAANC authorization" mentioned several times. So, what is it? LAANC stands for **L**ow **A**ltitude **A**uthorization and **N**otification **C**apability. It is the FAA's system that gives drone pilots fast, often instant, automated approval to fly in controlled airspace.*

Think of it as the modern, app-based way to get the permission you need. Don't worry about the specific apps or how to use them just yet—we'll cover that in detail in the "Tools of the Trade" section later in this lesson.

Understanding Altitude

Understanding altitude is critical. The FAA uses two different measurements, AGL and MSL, and you need to know which one applies to you. So, what's the difference?

1. **AGL (Above Ground Level):** This is your altitude measured directly from the ground beneath your drone. The 400-foot maximum altitude for drone pilots is **400 feet AGL**. If you take off from a 200-foot hill, your limit is still 400 feet directly above that hill.

2. **MSL (Mean Sea Level):** This is your true altitude measured from the average level of the ocean. All airport elevations and altitudes on sectional charts are given in **MSL**. Manned aircraft almost exclusively use MSL.

Why it matters: If you're standing on a hill with an elevation of 500 feet MSL, your drone flying at 400 feet AGL is actually at **900 feet MSL** (500 + 400). You need to understand this to correctly read airspace charts.

On a sectional chart, the "upside-down wedding cakes" for Class B and C airspace are shown with solid blue or magenta lines. The altitudes for each layer are written inside the circles.

Let's break down how to read the altitudes on the chart. They are displayed like a fraction and represent **hundreds of feet MSL**.

Think of it as: TOP of the airspace / BOTTOM of the airspace

- A number like **125 / SFC** means the airspace for that layer extends from the **Surface** up to **12,500 feet MSL**. This is the central core of the airport.

- A number like **125 / 30** in the next ring out means that layer's airspace starts at **3,000 feet MSL** (the floor) and goes up to **12,500 feet MSL** (the ceiling).

As a drone pilot, the bottom number is the most important. In the 125 / 30 example, the controlled airspace doesn't start until 3,000 feet MSL. This means the airspace from the ground up to 2,999 feet MSL is likely Class G or E, where you may be able to fly.

PRACTICAL EXAMPLE: Let's Figure out the Airspace

Take a look at the sectional chart image below again. You should now easily be able to pick out some airports, understand the airspace surrounding them and can describe their location by using the latitude and longitude.

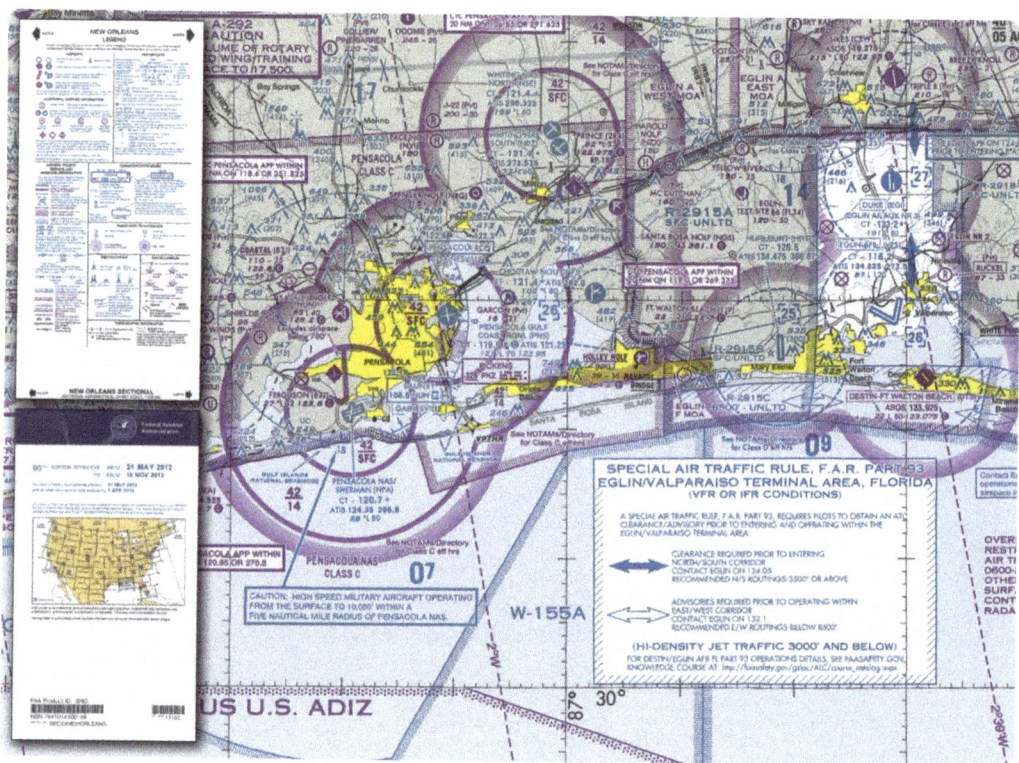

Figure 2.6. Sectional Chart and Legend. (Source: FAA-G-8082-22, Figure 11-2)

Where can you fly?

The easiest way to understand it is to separate the airspace into two simple groups: places you can fly freely and places where you need permission.

Where You Can Fly WITHOUT Permission

This is uncontrolled airspace, where you are free to fly up to 400 feet AGL without needing to contact Air Traffic Control.

On a sectional chart, you are in this "Go for it" airspace when:

- **There are no colored lines:** If your location is not inside any of the blue or magenta circles or lines, you are in **Class G** airspace.

- **You are under the "fuzzy" lines:** When you see a wide, fuzzy-edged **blue** or **magenta** line, it means the controlled **Class E** airspace starts high above you (at 1,200 ft or 700 ft AGL, respectively). As a drone pilot flying at or below 400 feet, you are safely in the Class G airspace underneath it and do not need authorization.

Where You Can Fly ONLY WITH Permission

This is controlled airspace that extends down to the surface. You **must** get authorization, typically through **LAANC**, before flying here.

You are in a "permission required" zone if your location is inside any of the following:

- **Solid Blue Lines** (Class B)

- **Solid Magenta Lines** (Class C)

- **Dashed Blue Lines** (Class D)

- **Dashed Magenta Lines** (Class E at the surface)

In short: If you're inside any solid or dashed line circle, you need LAANC. If you're outside of them, you're good to go.

Obstacles and Towers

As a drone pilot, you operate "down in the weeds" where most of the man-made obstructions live. Towers, antennas, and buildings are your primary collision risks, and the sectional chart is your best tool for identifying them *before* you fly. Knowing how to read these symbols isn't just for the test—it's a fundamental part of a safe flight plan.

Decoding the Obstacle Symbols

The FAA uses a few standard tower symbols to mark potential hazards on the chart.

Obstructions Over 1000ft AGL (Above Ground Level)

One Obstruction

One Obstruction with high-intensity lights

Multiple Obstructions

Obstructions Under 1000ft AGL (Above Ground Level)

One Obstruction

One Obstruction with high-intensity lights

Multiple Obstructions

Next to the tower symbols you will see a number like this.

2049
(1149)
UC

•Bold Number: The height of the obstruction in feet MSL (Mean Sea Level).

•Parentheses Number: The height of the obstruction in feet AGL (Above Ground Level).

•UC means under construction

Why it matters: Your 400-foot altitude limit is measured AGL, so the number in parentheses is the one you need to pay the most attention to.

The Invisible Threat: Guy Wires

Many tall, thin towers (especially communications towers) are supported by guy wires–thin steel cables that anchor the tower to the ground. These wires can extend hundreds of feet out from the base of the tower and are **virtually invisible** from the air. They are a significant and well-known hazard to all low-flying aircraft.

Crucial Safety Note: While the tower itself is marked on the chart, the **guy wires are not**. Never fly close to a charted tower, and always assume that guy wires are present, extending much farther than you think. A collision with a guy wire is almost always catastrophic.

Test Your Knowledge: Finding Obstacles

Take a look at the sectional chart below, you should now easily be able to pick out some obstructions with finding the tower symbols you just learned. See if you can tell where they are and how high they are.

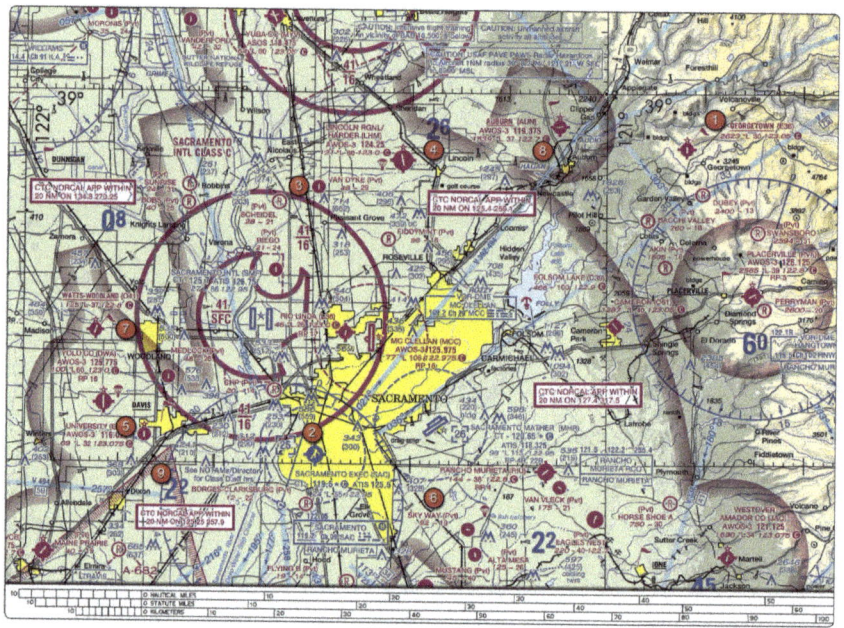

Figure 2.7. Sectional Chart Excerpt. (Source: FAA-G-8082-22, Figure 71)

The Big Numbers: Maximum Elevation Figure (MEF)

You'll notice that the sectional chart is divided into a grid of quadrants, and in the center of each quadrant are large, bold numbers. These are the **Maximum Elevation Figures (MEF)**, and they are one of the most important safety features on the chart.

Think of the MEF as a "quick glance" safety number for that entire grid square. It tells you the highest possible altitude of any feature—whether it's a mountain, a tower, or an antenna—within that box, measured in **feet MSL (Mean Sea Level)**.

- The large number represents thousands of feet.

- The small number represents hundreds of feet.

So, a large **1** followed by a small **2** in the middle of this chart means the highest point in that quadrant is **1,200 feet MSL**. The FAA calculates this by finding the highest feature and then rounding up to the next 100 feet for an added safety buffer.

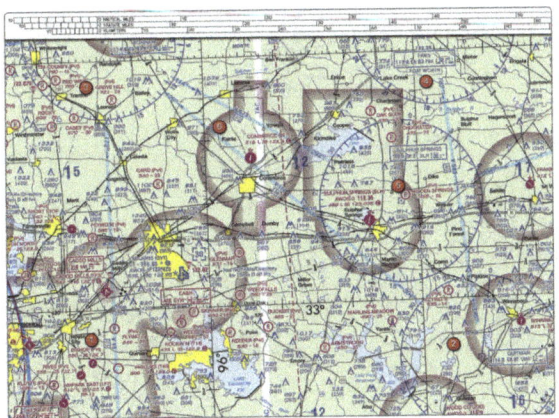

Figure 2.8. Sectional Chart and Legend.
(Source: FAA-G-8082-22, Figure 24)

Why This Matters: While your drone will be flying well below this altitude, the MEF gives you immediate situational awareness. A high MEF tells you instantly that you are operating in an area with high terrain or very tall obstacles, signaling that you need to be extra cautious and check the chart for the specific AGL height of any towers before you fly.

Test Your Knowledge: Finding Elevation Figures

Take a look at **Figure 2.9**, you should now easily see the quadrants and their Maximum Elevation Figures. You can see how they align with the elevation color chart on the upper right. Which quadrant is 6600 feet MSL?

Reading the Terrain: What the Colors Mean

The colors on a sectional chart tell you about the landscape below. The most important color for a drone pilot to recognize is **yellow**.

Yellow shaded areas represent populated places—cities, towns, and other congested areas. The FAA tints these areas yellow to give pilots an immediate visual warning that they are flying over a more densely populated location.

Why This Matters: For you as a remote pilot, these yellow areas are a major heads-up. They instantly tell you two critical things:

1. **Increased Risk:** Flying over a yellow-tinted area means there's a higher likelihood of people, cars, and buildings below.

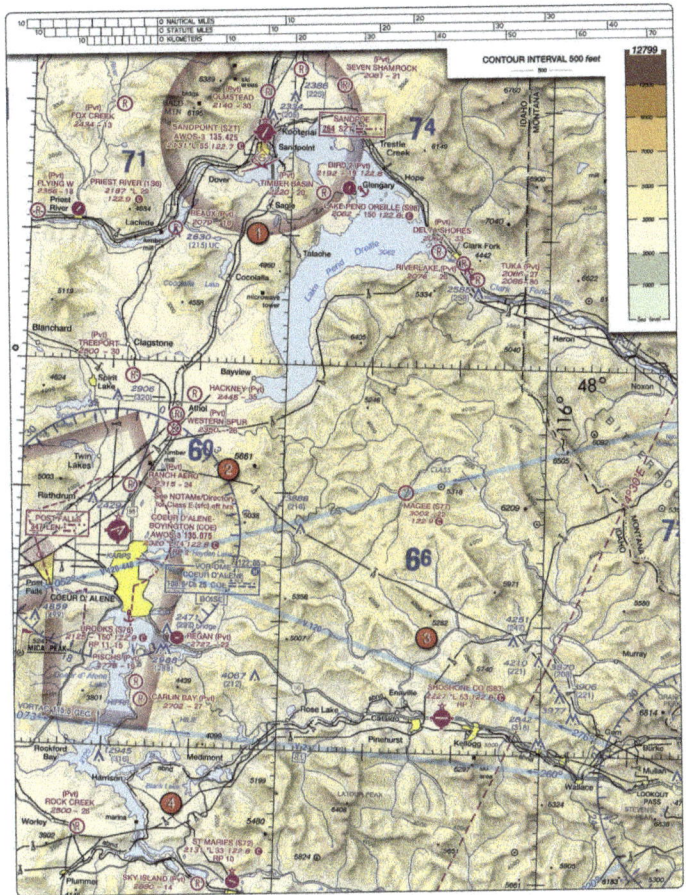

Figure 2.9. Sectional Chart and Legend. (Source: FAA-G-8082-22, Figure 22)

2. **Operations Over People Rules Apply:** When you see yellow, you must be extra vigilant in making sure your flight complies with one of the four categories for flying over people.

Essentially, the yellow shading is a clear signal to slow down, increase your awareness, and double-check the rules before you launch.

Special Use Airspace – Know the Boundaries

Beyond the main airspace classes, you will also see special zones on the chart marked with hashed lines. It is critical to know what these are.

Prohibited Areas (P-###)

Think "Keep Out!" Flying in a Prohibited Area is completely forbidden for all aircraft. These are established for national security, like over the White House, Camp David or any other places that wouldn't normally allow aircraft.

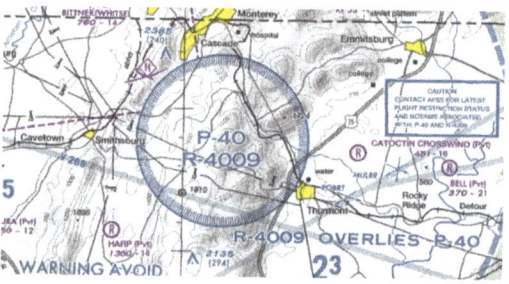

Figure 2.10. An example of a prohibited area, P-40 around Camp David. (Source: FAA-G-8082-22, Figure 2-2)

Restricted Areas (R-###)

Think "Enter with Permission." Flight in these areas is restricted due to hazardous activities, like artillery firing or guided missile tests. You cannot fly in a Restricted Area when it's "active" without getting specific permission from the controlling agency. The chart will tell you the altitudes and active times.

Figure 2.11. Restricted areas on a sectional chart. (Source: FAA-G-8082-22, Figure 2-3)

Warning Areas (W-###)

These are similar to Restricted Areas but are located over international waters (starting 3 nautical miles offshore). The U.S. doesn't have the authority to restrict flight there, but they are warning you of hazardous activity.

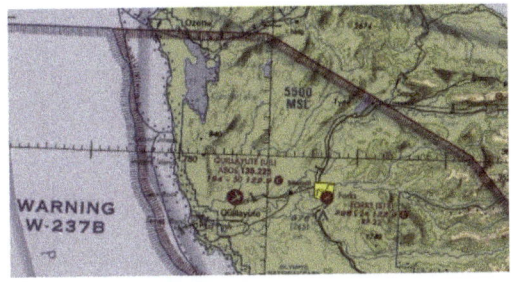

Figure 2.12. Requirements for airspace operations. (Source: FAA-G-8082-22, Figure 2-4)

Military Operations Areas (MOAs)

These are areas where military aircraft conduct training, often at high speeds and in acrobatic maneuvers. You *can* fly your drone in an MOA, but you must exercise extreme caution. It's always best to check the active times and avoid them if possible.

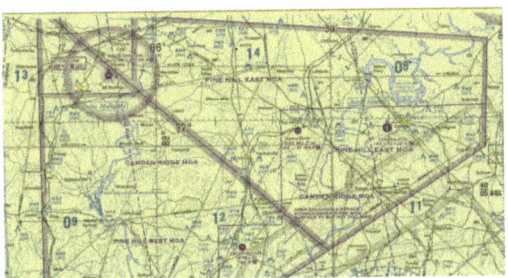

Figure 2.13. Camden Ridge MOA is an example of a military operations area. (Source: FAA-G-8082-22, Figure 2-5)

Alert Areas: (A-###)

These areas contain a high volume of pilot training or unusual aerial activity. Just like MOAs, you can fly in them, but you need to be extra alert for other aircraft.

Figure 2.14. Alert area (A-211). (Source: FAA-G-8082-22, Figure 2-6)

Test Your Knowledge: Finding Obstacles

Take a look at **Figure 2.15** below and see if you can spot Special Use Airspace and the populated areas.

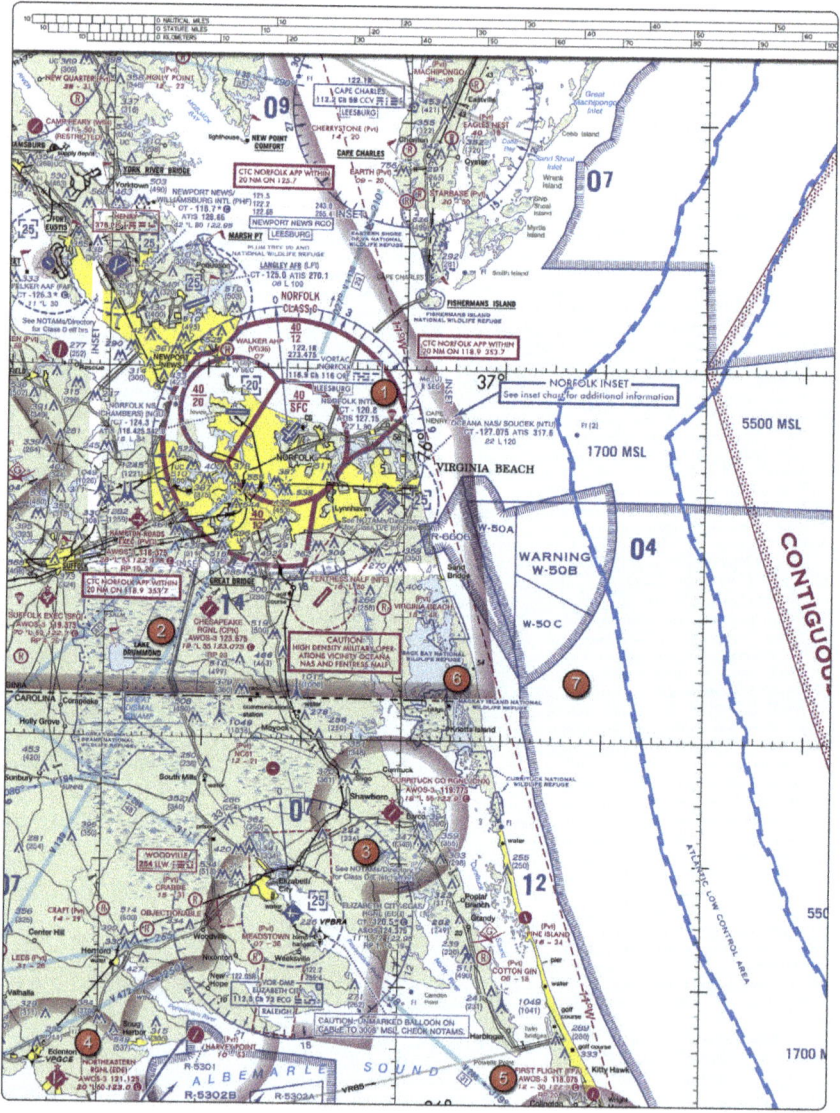

Figure 2.15. Sectional Chart Excerpt. (Source: FAA-CT-8080-2H, Figure 74)

Test You Knowledge: Bringing it all together

By understanding these four key areas—airspace classes, lat/long navigation, airport symbols, and obstacle heights—you'll be ready to answer nearly any sectional chart question on the exam and plan your real-world flights safely.

Take a look at **Figure 2.16**. Look familiar? It's the exact same chart we showed you at the beginning of the chapter. Looks different doesn't it? You should now be able to identify everything you'll need to know to pilot a drone and for the exam.

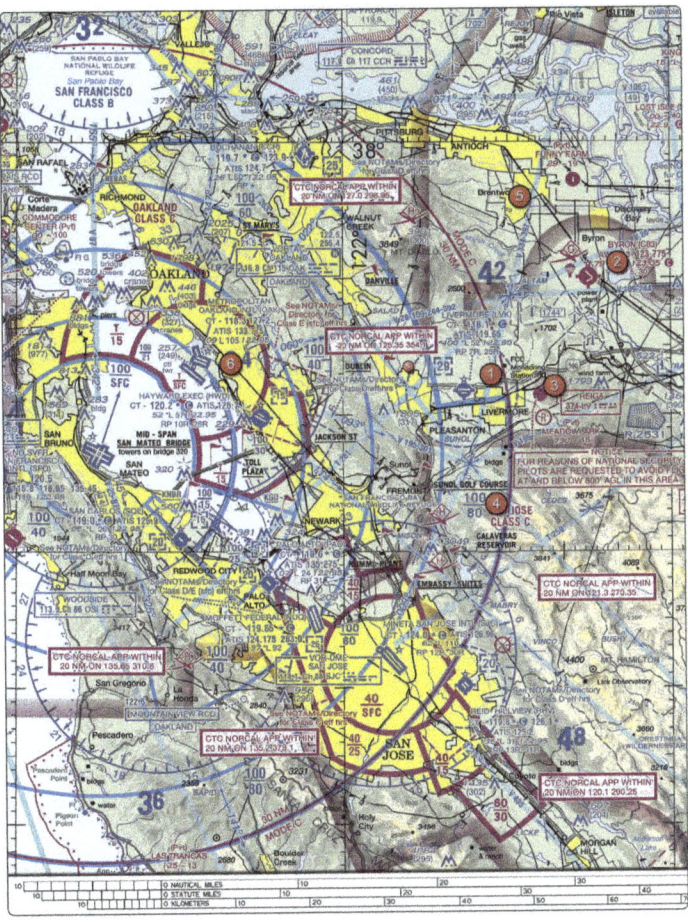

Figure 2.16. Sectional Chart Excerpt. (Source: FAA-CT-8080-2H, Figure 20)

The Master Key

We've covered all the critical symbols you need to know for your exam. However, the sectional chart is packed with much more information. On test day, you will be given a testing supplement that contains the full, official FAA Sectional Chart Legend, which looks like this:

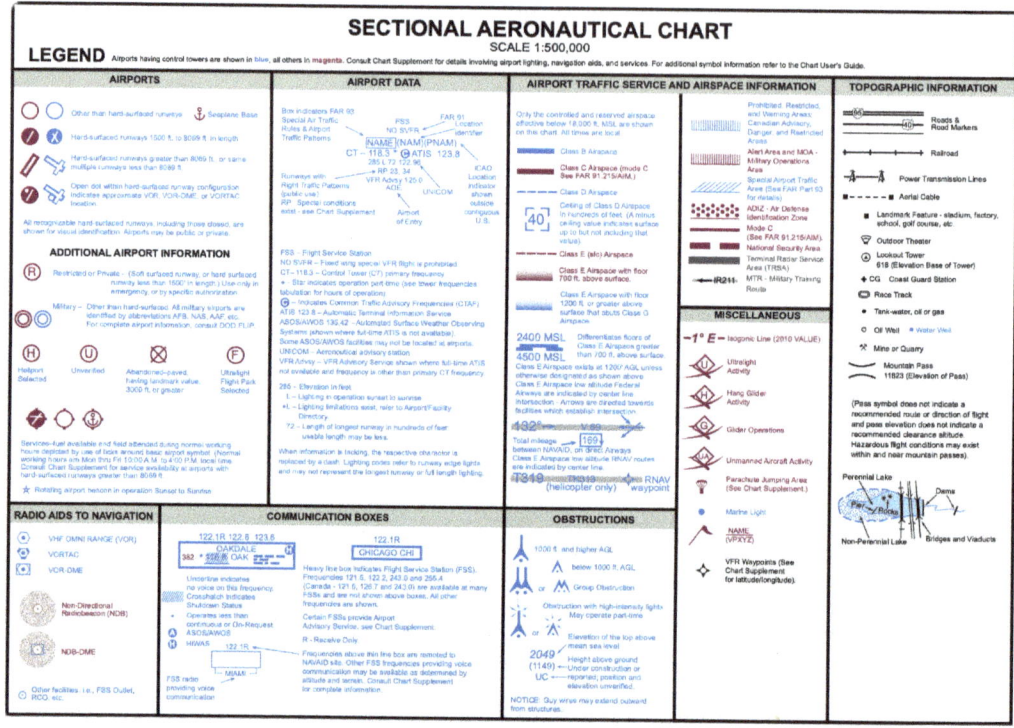

Figure 2.17. Sectional Aeronautical Chart Legend. (Source: FAA-CT-8080-2H, Legend 1)

You absolutely do **not** need to memorize everything on this page. However, you should be aware that this complete legend exists in the testing supplement. If you encounter a rare or unfamiliar symbol during the exam—like a parachute jumping area or a glider operations area—don't panic. You have the official guide right at your fingertips. Take the time to look it up.

Tools of the Trade: Getting Information and Authorization

Knowing the rules is one thing; having the right tools to apply them in the field is another. Here are the essential apps and services you'll use as a professional drone pilot.

- **B4UFLY: Your Situational Awareness Tool**
  B4UFLY is the FAA's program for providing pilots with real-time airspace information. However, the FAA doesn't make the app itself anymore. Instead, they have approved several private companies to provide B4UFLY services through their own apps. As of late 2024, the official providers include **Airspace Link, Aloft, AutoPylot, Avision, and UASidekick**. These apps are excellent for a quick check of your surroundings.

- **LAANC: Your Key to Instant Authorization**
  For airspace authorization in controlled airspace (B, C, D, and some E), your primary tool is the **Low Altitude Authorization and Notification Capability (LAANC)**. This is the system that provides near-instant, automated approvals for flights at pre-approved altitudes shown on the UAS Facility Maps. The same companies that provide B4UFLY services are also approved LAANC providers. You will use their apps to submit your request and get approval, often in seconds.

- **DroneZone: The Manual Backup**
  The FAA's DroneZone website is where you go when LAANC can't handle your request. You'll use DroneZone if:

  - LAANC isn't available at the airport or controlled airspace you want to fly in.

  - You need to request an altitude higher than the LAANC facility map allows.

  - Your operation requires manual FAA review (special circumstances or complex missions).

  - You're applying for long-term or recurring authorizations (e.g., flying the same site for months).

Unlike LAANC, DroneZone approvals are not instant and may take several days to weeks—so plan ahead. DroneZone is also used for drone registration, renewals, and waivers (such as BVLOS or flying over people).

Your Drone's Built-in Guardian Angel

You might be wondering, "If I'm not supposed to fly near an airport, won't my drone just stop me?" The answer is, most likely, yes. The truth of the matter is, major manufacturers like DJI build in a system called **geofencing**.

Think of it as an invisible, GPS-based fence around sensitive locations like airports, military bases, and national parks. The term comes from combining "geographic" and "fence." If you try to fly your drone into one of these restricted zones, the drone's software will often stop automatically, preventing you from entering the airspace.

So why do you still need to learn all the airspace rules? Because **you**, the Remote Pilot in Command, are ultimately responsible, not the software. Geofencing is a fantastic safety backup, but it's not foolproof. The database might not be up-to-date with a temporary flight restriction (TFR), or you might be flying a drone that doesn't have the feature. The law requires *you* to know the rules, and you can never use "my drone let me do it" as an excuse.

Key Takeaways

- Know the primary airspace classes: **B, C, D, E, and G.**

- Remember the color codes: **Blue** symbols for towered airports, **Magenta** for non-towered.

- Obstacle heights are shown in both Mean Sea Level (**MSL**) and Above Ground Level (**AGL**). Your 400-foot limit is AGL.

- **Class G** is uncontrolled airspace and has no specific chart markings; you are in it by process of elimination.

Likely Exam Questions:

1. What does a dashed magenta line indicate?

2. What's the AGL height of an obstacle if MSL is 2,154 ft and AGL is 300 ft?

3. What airspace is indicated by a solid magenta line?

4. In which class of airspace can most drones fly without ATC authorization?

5. How would you locate 35°15'N, 97°25'W on a sectional chart?

Weather Wizards

How Weather Affects Your Drone

Now that you know the rules of the road and where you can fly, it's time to talk about something that can change your flight plans in an instant: the weather. As a drone pilot, you're also a part-time meteorologist. Understanding weather isn't just for passing the test—it's one of the most critical skills for being a safe and effective pilot.

The Engine of Weather

The primary cause of every weather phenomenon, from a gentle breeze to a raging hurricane, is caused by one single thing: **the sun unevenly heating the surface of the Earth**.

Because the Earth is tilted and curved, the sun's rays hit the equator directly, making it hot. The poles receive sunlight at an angle, making them cold. This temperature difference creates a massive, constant struggle for balance in our atmosphere, and that struggle is what we call "weather."

How Air Moves

The result of this uneven heating is a simple process: **warm air rises, and cool air sinks**.

Think about a hot air balloon. You heat the air inside, it becomes less dense than the surrounding air, and it rises. The same thing happens in the atmosphere every day. When the sun heats the ground, the air just above it gets warm, less dense, and begins to rise. Higher up, the air is colder and denser, so it sinks to take the place of the rising warm air. This continuous circulation of rising warm air and sinking cool air is called **convection**, and it's the engine that drives wind, clouds, and storms.

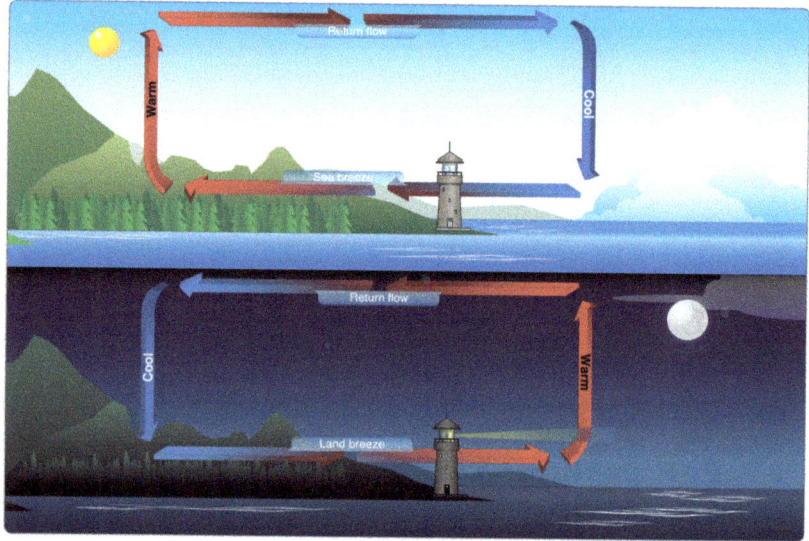

Figure 3.1. Sea breeze and land breeze wind circulation patterns. (Source: FAA-H-8083-25C, Figure 11-3)

Figure 3.1 shows how the different heating and cooling rates of land and water create predictable daily wind patterns known as **sea breezes** and **land breezes**. The key principle is that land heats up and cools down much faster than water.

Daytime: Sea Breeze (Top Panel)

1. **Sun Heats Land:** During the day, the sun quickly heats the land.

2. **Warm Air Rises:** The air over the warm land heats up, becomes less dense, and rises. This creates an area of lower pressure over the land.

3. **Cool Air Sinks:** The water stays cooler, so the air above it remains cool, dense, and sinks, creating higher pressure.

4. **Wind Blows Inland:** To fill the low-pressure gap over the land, the cool, high-pressure air from the sea blows inland. This is the **sea breeze**.

Nighttime: Land Breeze (Bottom Panel)

1. **Land Cools Down:** At night, the land loses its heat rapidly and becomes colder than the water, which retains its warmth.

2. **Warm Air Rises (Over Water):** Now, the air over the warmer water is rising, creating lower pressure over the sea.

3. **Cool Air Sinks (Over Land):** The air over the cool land also cools, becomes dense, and sinks, creating higher pressure.

4. **Wind Blows to Sea:** To fill the gap over the water, the cool, high-pressure air from the land blows out to sea. This is the **land breeze**.

Why It Matters for a Drone Pilot

This creates a predictable daily cycle of wind in coastal areas. You can expect the wind to blow **from the ocean** during the day and **from the land** at night. Knowing this helps you plan your flights, anticipate wind direction, and manage your battery life more effectively.

What is Wind?

Wind is simply the atmosphere trying to balance itself out. As warm air rises, it leaves behind an area of lower pressure. When cool air sinks, it creates an area of higher pressure. Air always flows from high pressure to low pressure, and we call this movement **wind**. The greater the pressure difference, the stronger the wind.

How Wind Affects Your Drone: This is the biggest weather factor for drone pilots. Strong winds can make it difficult to control your drone, drain your battery significantly faster as the motors fight to hold position, and in severe cases, can lead to a "flyaway" where you lose the drone altogether.

Thermals: Invisible Elevators

A **thermal** is a column of rising warm air caused by localized heating of the ground, like over a dark parking lot or a rocky field. For a small, lightweight drone, flying through a thermal can feel like hitting a speed bump. It can cause a sudden updraft, making the flight bumpy and requiring the pilot to make control inputs to maintain altitude. While not usually dangerous, it's a form of turbulence you should be aware of.

Wind Shear: A Sudden Threat

Wind shear is a sudden, drastic change in wind speed and/or direction over a very short distance. It can flip a drone or make it completely uncontrollable. Wind shear doesn't only happen during storms. It can occur on perfectly clear days when the wind interacts with objects on the ground.

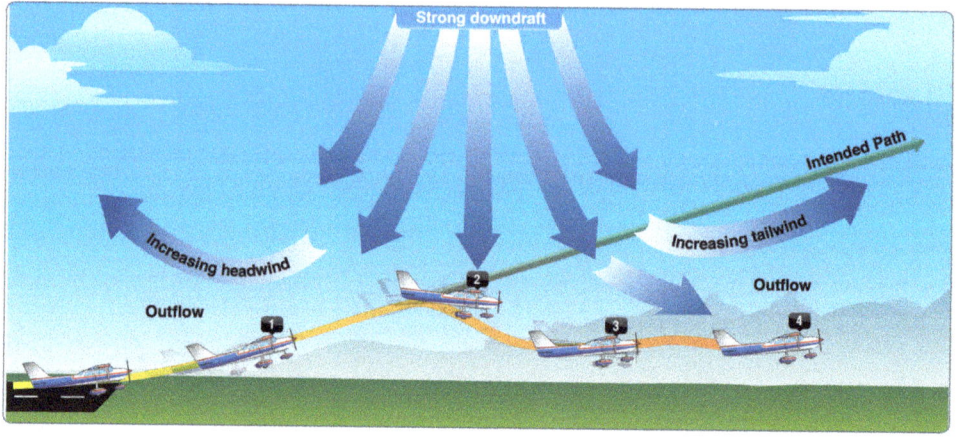

Figure 3.2. Effects of a microburst wind. (Source: FAA-H-8083-25C, Figure 12-17)

Think of the wind as water flowing in a river. When it hits a large rock, the water becomes chaotic and turbulent on the other side. Air behaves the same way as shown in **Figure 3.3**.

Figure 3.3. Turbulence caused by manmade obstructions. (Source: FAA-H-8083-25C, Figure 12-15)

When wind flows over or around obstacles like a line of trees, a large building, or a hill, it creates invisible pockets of rough, swirling air on the **downwind side** (the side sheltered from the wind). See **Figure 3.4**. For a drone, flying into this turbulence can cause a sudden drop or loss of control.

It is especially dangerous because it's often invisible and can occur in several places:

- **Near thunderstorms**, as downdrafts create powerful, unpredictable gusts.

- **Near the ground on windy days** due to friction with terrain and obstacles.

- **During a temperature inversion**, where a layer of warm air sits on top of a layer of cold air.

Figure 3.4. Turbulence caused by manmade obstructions. (Source: FAA-H-8083-25C, Figure 12-16)

Dew Point and Fog

Dew point is the temperature at which the air becomes completely saturated and can no longer hold all of its water vapor. When the air temperature cools down to meet the dew point, the invisible water vapor condenses into visible water droplets.

Fog is simply a cloud that forms at the surface. It happens when the temperature and dew point become very close or identical.

- **Relevance for Drone Pilots:** Fog is a major hazard. It dramatically reduces visibility, making it impossible to maintain the required Visual Line-of-Sight (VLOS). Flying in fog can also introduce moisture into your drone's electronics, risking damage or failure. If you see the temperature and dew point are close in a weather report, be prepared for potential fog.

Clouds

Clouds form through the same process as fog, just higher up. As a parcel of warm, moist air rises, it expands and cools. When it cools to its dew point, the water vapor condenses into tiny droplets or ice crystals, forming a visible cloud.

Cloud Classifications and What They Mean

Clouds are generally classified by their appearance and altitude. Knowing the basic types helps you predict the weather.

- **Stratus Clouds:** These are flat, featureless, layered clouds that form in stable air. They look like sheets covering the sky and often bring drizzle and poor visibility. If you see stratus clouds, expect gloomy conditions.

- **Cumulus Clouds:** These are the puffy, cotton-like clouds with flat bases that form in unstable air. They are a sign of updrafts (thermals). Fair-weather cumulus clouds signal good flying conditions, but if they start growing vertically, they can turn into...

- **Cumulonimbus Clouds:** These are thunderstorm clouds. They are massive, towering clouds that bring severe turbulence, lightning, hail, and extreme wind shear. **Never fly a drone anywhere near a cumulonimbus cloud.**

Microburst clues: Watch for **virga** (rain that evaporates before reaching the ground) and a **ring of blowing dust** at the surface—both are classic signs of damaging outflow winds.

The Golden Rule: Cloud Clearance

Under Part 107, your drone must stay a minimum distance away from all clouds. This ensures you can see and avoid manned aircraft that might be flying in or near them. The rule is:

- 500 feet below any cloud.

- 2,000 feet horizontally from any cloud.

Air Stability

The stability of the air is a summary of all these concepts. It tells you what to expect from the weather.

- **Stable Air:** In stable air, rising air is discouraged. This leads to:

    - **Clouds:** Stratus (flat layers).

    - **Visibility:** Poor, with haze and smoke trapped near the ground.

    - **Precipitation:** Steady drizzle.

    - **Air:** Smooth.

- **Unstable Air:** In unstable air, rising air is encouraged (thermals). This leads to:

    - **Clouds:** Cumulus (puffy, towering).

    - **Visibility:** Good, except in areas of precipitation.

    - **Precipitation:** Showery, with thunderstorms possible.

    - **Air:** Turbulent (bumpy).

Hazardous Weather to Watch For

Beyond the basics of wind and rain, the FAA exam requires you to understand a few specific weather hazards:

- **Thunderstorms:** A thunderstorm isn't just rain; it's a weather-making machine. Every thunderstorm has three stages in its life cycle (See **Figure 3.5**):

  1. **Cumulus Stage:** The storm is building. You'll see strong updrafts of air.

  2. **Mature Stage:** This is the most dangerous stage. You will experience both updrafts and downdrafts, heavy rain, and lightning. This is also when hail is most likely to form.

  3. **Dissipating Stage:** The storm is weakening, and you'll see mostly downdrafts.

  The Rule: Never fly near a thunderstorm. The powerful winds can be hazardous for many miles around the storm itself.

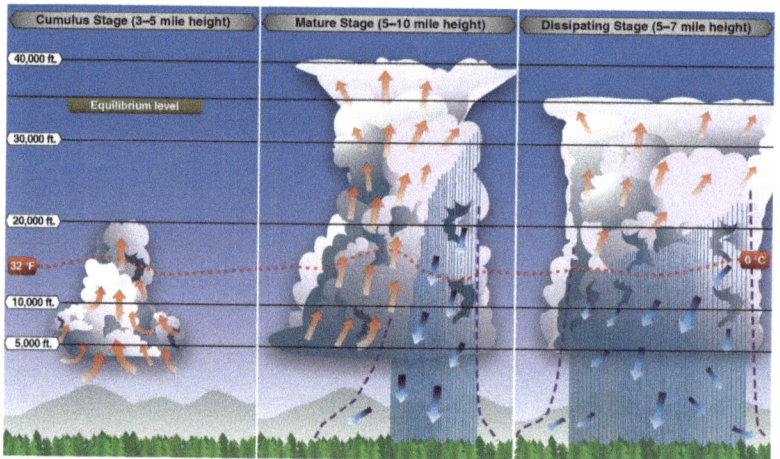

Figure 3.5. Life cycle of a thunderstorm (FAA-G-8082-22), Figure 3-4)

- **Wind Shear:** This is a sudden, drastic change in wind speed and/or direction over a very short distance. It can happen at any altitude but is especially dangerous near the ground. Wind shear can be caused by thunderstorms, temperature inversions, or even weather fronts. It can easily cause you to lose control of your drone.

- **Structural Icing:** Drones are not certified to fly in icing conditions. If you fly through visible moisture (like clouds or rain) when the temperature is at or below freezing (0°C / 32°F), ice can form on your drone's propellers and frame. This disrupts the flow of air, adds weight, and can quickly lead to a loss of lift and a crash.

Reading the Weather: METARs and TAFs

So, how do you know what the weather is going to be like? You'll need to learn how to read a few special weather reports that pilots use. The two most important ones are **METARs** and **TAFs**. METAR is current weather and TAF is the forecasted weather.

METAR (Meteorological Aerodrome Report)

This is a report of the current weather conditions at an airport. It's typically updated every hour, but if weather conditions change rapidly, an unscheduled special report called a **SPECI** will be issued.

Here's a METAR example.

```
METAR KINK 121845Z 11012G18KT 15SM SKC 25/17 A3000

METAR KBOI 121854Z 13004KT 30SM SCT150 17/6 A3015

METAR KLAX 121852Z 25004KT 6SM BR SCT007 SCT250 16/15 A2991

SPECI KMDW 121856Z 32005KT 1 1/2SM RA OVC007 17/16 A2980 RMK RAB35

SPECI KJFK 121853Z 18004KT 1/2SM FG R04/2200 OVC005 20/18 A3006
```

Figure 3.6. Aviation Routine Weather Reports METAR (Source: FAA-CT-8080-2H, Figure 11-3)

TAF (Terminal Aerodrome Forecast)

This is a forecast of the weather conditions at an airport for the next 24 to 30 hours. It's like a METAR, but for the future. They are given 4 times a day in Zulu time at 00Z, 06Z, 12Z, and 18Z.

Here's an example of a TAF:

```
TAF

KMEM 121720Z 1218/1324 20012KT 5SM HZ BKN030 PROB40 1220/1222 1SM TSRA OVC008CB
     FM122200 33015G20KT P6SM BKN015 OVC025 PROB40 1220/1222 3SM SHRA
     FM120200 35012KT OVC008 PROB40 1202/1205 2SM-RASN BECMG 1306/1308 02008KT BKN012
     BECMG 1310/1312 00000KT 3SM BR SKC TEMPO 1212/1214 1/2SM FG
     FM131600 VRB06KT P6SM SKC=

KOKC 051130Z 0512/0618 14008KT 5SM BR BKN030 TEMPO 0513/0516 1 1/2SM BR
     FM051600 18010KT P6SM SKC BECMG 0522/0524 20013G20KT 4SM SHRA OVC020
     PROB40 0600/0606 2SM TSRA OVC008CB BECMG 0606/0608 21015KT P6SM SCT040=
```

Figure 3.7. Terminal Aerodrome Forecasts TAF (Source: FAA-CT-8080-2H, Figure 15)

Just remember, **METAR** is the weather right now and **TAF** is the forecasted weather.

Let's decode a real METAR and TAF, piece by piece.

METAR Example: KLAX 121852Z 25004KT 6SM BR SCT007 SCT250 16/15 A2991

- **KLAX:** The is the station identifier where the observation was taken. K means it's a U.S. based airport and LAX is the airport code. So the was from LAX, Los Angeles International Airport.

- **121852Z:** Date and time the observation was made. Issued on the 12th day of the month at 1852 Zulu time. Zulu time is UTC time and perfect for air travel because it never changes.

- **25004KT:** Wind direction (where the wind is coming from) and wind speed. From 250 degrees at 4 knots. Sometimes you may see a variation of this like **25004KTG30KT**. This means the wind is coming from 250 degrees at 4 knots with gusts up to 30 knots.

- **6SM:** Visibility. 6 statute miles.

- **BR:** Weather phenomenon. BR stands for Mist. (FG would be Fog, DZ for Drizzle, RA for Rain, TS for Thunderstorm).

- **SCT007 SCT250:** Cloud cover. Scattered clouds at 700 feet AGL and another scattered layer at 25,000 feet AGL. This section can have multiple laters. (SKC/CLR would be Sky Clear / Clear, FEW Few Clouds, SCT = Scattered Clouds, BKN = Broken Clouds,, OVC = Overcast, VV = Vertical Visibility)

- **16/15:** Temperature and Dew Point in Celsius. 16°C and 15°C. When the temperature and dew point are close, expect fog or low clouds.

- **A2991:** Altimeter setting. 29.91 inHg which stands for inches of mercury. This is the atmospheric pressure at sea level. This is helpful for pilots to calibrate their altitude gauges.

Sometimes after the Altimeter setting, you'll see an additional **RMK**. This stands for Remark which may contain additional information after the standard METAR report. There's so much more to METAR reports, but you now have a basic understanding and all the knowledge you'll need for the exam.

Now let's move on to an example of a TAF Report.

TAF Example: TAF KMEM 121720Z 1218/1324 20012KT 5SM HZ BKN030 FM122200 33015G20KT P6SM SKC TEMPO 1220/1223 1/2SM FG BECMG 1306/1308 02008KT

- **KMEM:** ICAO airport identifier, which is Memphis.

- **121720Z:** Issued the 12th day at 17:20 Zulu time.

- **1218/1324:** Forecast valid from the 12th day at 1800Z until the 13th day at 2400Z.

- **20012KT:** Wind from 200 degrees at 12 knots

- **5SM:** 5 miles visibility

- **HZ BKN030:** Haze, Broken clouds at 3,000 feet.

- **FM122200 33015G20KT...: FM** stands for **FROM** the 12th day of the month at 2200Z, the weather will permanently change to: Wind from 330 at 15 knots gusting to 20

- **TEMPO 1212/1214 1/2SM FG: TEMPO** means **TEMPORARILY**. Between 1200Z and 1400Z on the 12th, conditions may temporarily become 1/2 mile visibility in Fog.

- **BECMG 1306/1308 02008KT: BECMG** means **BECOMING**. Between 0600Z and 0800Z on the 13th, the weather will gradually change to the new conditions (wind from 020 degrees at 8 knots)

A Note on Studying for the Test

Now that you've seen how to decode these reports, two big questions probably come to mind:

1. **Will I actually have to know this for the test? Yes, absolutely.** You are guaranteed to see several questions on the Part 107 exam that require you to read and interpret METAR and TAF reports. The official Airman Certification Standards (ACS), which is the FAA's blueprint for the test, lists "Weather Sources and Effects" as a required knowledge area, and this specifically includes METARs and TAFs.

2. **Is there a guide given to me for this during the exam? No, there is not.** Unlike the sectional chart, the Airman Knowledge Testing Supplement that you are given during the exam **does not** include a legend or a decoder key for METAR and TAF abbreviations.

You are expected to have the common abbreviations (like BR for mist, HZ for haze, BKN for broken clouds, etc.) and the report structure memorized. This is why the detailed breakdown in this chapter is so important—it provides the exact knowledge you need to bring with you into the testing center.

Weather Resources

You don't have to be a meteorologist to get good weather information. There are plenty of great resources available to help you out.

How to Get an Official Briefing

While apps are great, the two primary sources for an official FAA weather briefing are:

- **1-800-WX-BRIEF:** You can call this number and speak directly to a flight weather briefer. You can tell them where and when you plan to fly, and they will give you a full report of current and expected weather conditions, including any relevant NOTAMs.

- **https://www.1800wxbrief.com/:** This is the official website that provides the same information online. You can get a standard briefing, check for NOTAMs, and even file a flight plan.

Other Great Tools

- **Aviation Weather Center (AWC):** This is the official source for aviation weather information from the National Weather Service at **https://aviationweather.gov**

- **Drone-specific weather apps:** There are many apps available that provide detailed weather forecasts specifically for drone pilots.

That's a quick look at how weather can affect your drone. The most important thing is to always check the weather before you fly and to be prepared for changing conditions. If the weather looks bad, don't be afraid to postpone your flight. A safe flight is always the best flight.

Key Takeaways

- A **METAR** is a report of *current* weather at an airport, while a **TAF** is a *forecast* for the next 24-30 hours.

- The biggest weather concerns for a drone pilot are **wind, temperature, visibility, and density altitude.**

- **Density altitude** is a critical performance measure; the "thinner" the air (higher elevation, hotter temperature), the worse your drone will perform.

Likely Test Questions

1. You need to check the current weather conditions for a flight this afternoon. Which type of report should you look at?

1. **(Refer to Figure 12)** What are the current wind conditions at KLAX?

2. What is density altitude?

3. How does high density altitude affect the performance of a small unmanned aircraft?

4. **(Refer to Figure 15)** In the TAF for KMEM, what weather conditions are forecast to happen temporarily between 1200Z and 1400Z on the 12th?

Understanding Drone Performance

Pushing the Limits

Welcome back, Red Raven aviator! We've covered the rules, the airspace, and how to talk the talk. Now let's get into the nitty-gritty of what your drone can actually do. Every drone is different, and understanding its unique performance capabilities is key to being a safe and effective pilot.

Think of your drone like a car. You wouldn't try to drive a small city car up a steep, icy mountain road. In the same way, you need to know the limits of your drone before you send it on a challenging mission.

Your Drone's Bible: The Pilot's Operating Handbook (POH)

How do you find out your drone's limits? You read its bible: the **Pilot's Operating Handbook (POH)** or flight manual. This document, created by the manufacturer, contains everything you need to know about your drone's performance.

It will tell you things like:

- **Max wind speed:** The strongest wind your drone can safely fly in.

- **Operating temperature range:** The hottest and coldest conditions your drone can handle.

- **Battery life:** How long you can expect to fly on a single charge (this is often an ideal number, so take it with a grain of salt!).

- **Max flight speed and climb rate:** How fast your drone can go.

Seriously, read this manual. It might not be as exciting as this guidebook, but it contains life-saving information about your specific drone model.

The Big Three: Factors Affecting Performance

Your drone's performance isn't static. It changes based on the conditions of the day. The three biggest factors you need to consider are **weather, weight, and density altitude.**

1. **Weather:** As we learned in Chapter 4, wind is a major player. A strong headwind will slow your drone down and drain your battery much faster. Flying in temperatures outside the recommended range can also drastically reduce battery life and potentially damage your drone.

2. **Weight:** This one is simple physics. The heavier your drone is, the harder the motors have to work. Adding a bigger camera or a special sensor will reduce your flight time and make the drone less agile. Always stay under that 55 lb limit and be aware that a heavier drone will feel different in the air.

3. **Density Altitude:** This is the performance killer that many new pilots forget about. Density altitude is a measure of how "thick" or dense the air is. The air becomes less dense when:

   - You're at a **higher elevation** (e.g., flying in the mountains).

   - The temperature is hotter.

   - The humidity is higher.

   Why does this matter? Your drone's propellers work by "grabbing" air. When the air is less dense, the propellers have less to grab onto. This means the motors have to spin much faster to generate the same amount of lift. This results in:

   - Reduced climb performance.

   - Shorter flight times.

   - Less responsive controls.

You might be able to fly for 25 minutes in cool, dry air at sea level, but that same drone might only fly for 18 minutes on a hot, humid day in Denver. Always account for density altitude in your flight planning!

4. **Load Factor:** This is the extra stress, or "G-force," placed on your drone whenever you're not flying straight and level. In a steep turn, for example, your drone's wings (or propellers) have to create more lift to fight the turn's centrifugal force, making the drone "feel" much heavier. In a 60-degree bank turn, the load factor is 2 Gs, meaning your drone and all its components are experiencing twice their normal weight in stress. Pushing your drone into aggressive maneuvers can over-stress the airframe and motors, and will dramatically decrease your battery life.

Test Your Knowledge: Using the Density Altitude Chart

Let's walk through a real-world scenario to see how this chart works.

Scenario: You are preparing for a flight in the mountains. The airport elevation is **4,000 feet**, the current altimeter setting is **29.42 "Hg**, and the outside air temperature is a hot **90°F**. What is the actual density altitude your drone will be performing in?

Step 1: Find the Pressure Altitude. First, you need to correct for the non-standard pressure. Look at the "Pressure altitude conversion factor" table on the right. Find the altimeter setting of **29.40** (the closest value to 29.42), which corresponds to a conversion factor of **+485 feet**.

- Airport Elevation + Conversion Factor = Pressure Altitude

- 4,000 ft + 485 ft = 4,485 ft (Pressure Altitude).

Step 2: Find the Intersection on the Chart.

1. Find the outside air temperature of **90°F** along the bottom axis of the main chart.

2. Find the pressure altitude of **4,500 feet** (the closest line to our calculated 4,485 ft) on the vertical axis of the chart.

3. Follow the grid line up from 90°F and across from 4,500 feet until the two lines intersect.

Step 3: Read the Density Altitude. In **Figure 4.1**, from that intersection point, follow the nearest diagonal line up and to the left. You will see that the line points to approximately **7,500 feet**.

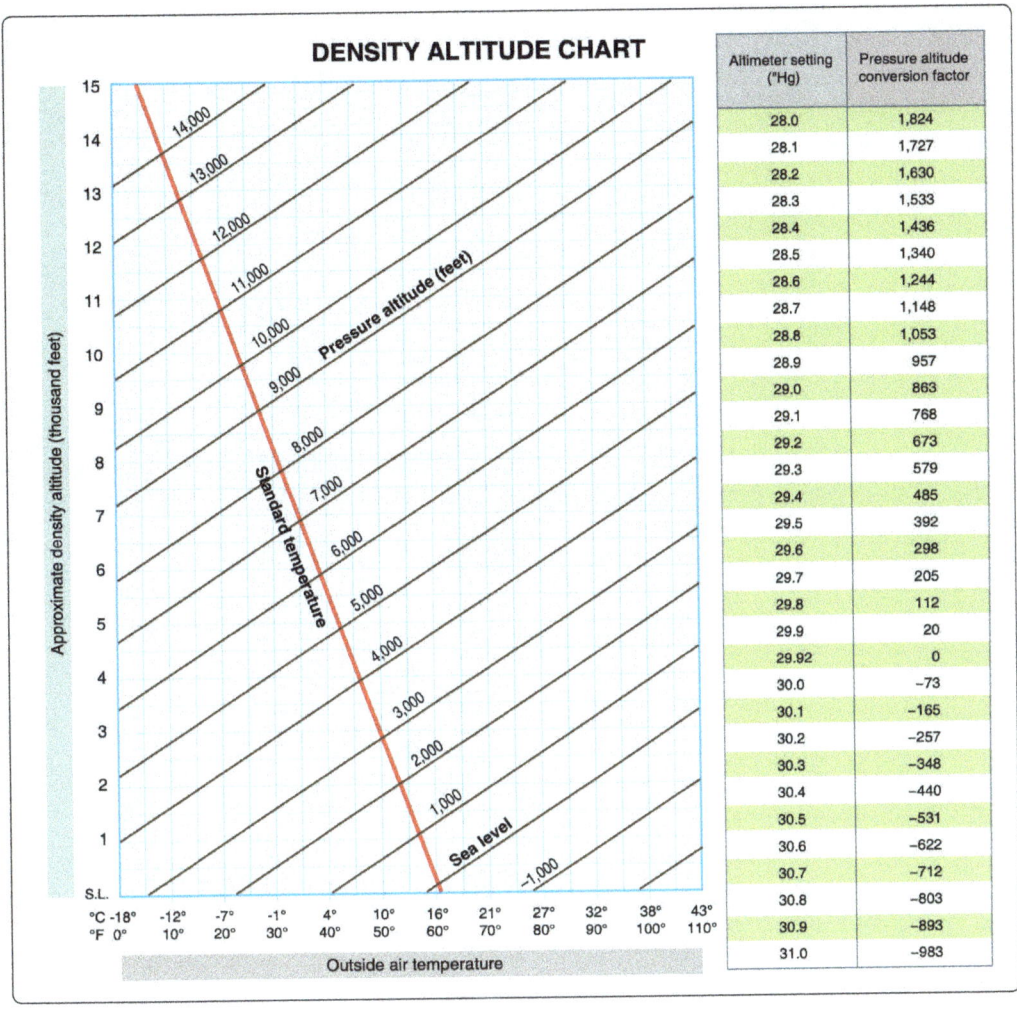

Figure 4.1. Density Altitude Chart (Source: FAA-CT-8080-2H, Figure 8)

Conclusion: Even though you are physically standing at 4,000 feet, the hot temperature and low pressure make the air so "thin" that your drone will perform as if it were at **7,500 feet**. This means you can expect significantly reduced performance and shorter flight times.

Decoding the Wind: Headwinds vs. Crosswinds

Knowing the wind speed is important, but knowing its direction relative to your takeoff and landing path is critical. Every drone has a maximum wind speed it can handle, but it also has a separate, much lower limit for how much **crosswind** it can tolerate. A crosswind is a wind that blows across your flight path, rather than directly at you (a headwind).

On the test, you may be required to calculate the headwind and crosswind components using an official FAA chart like the one below in **Figure 4.2**.

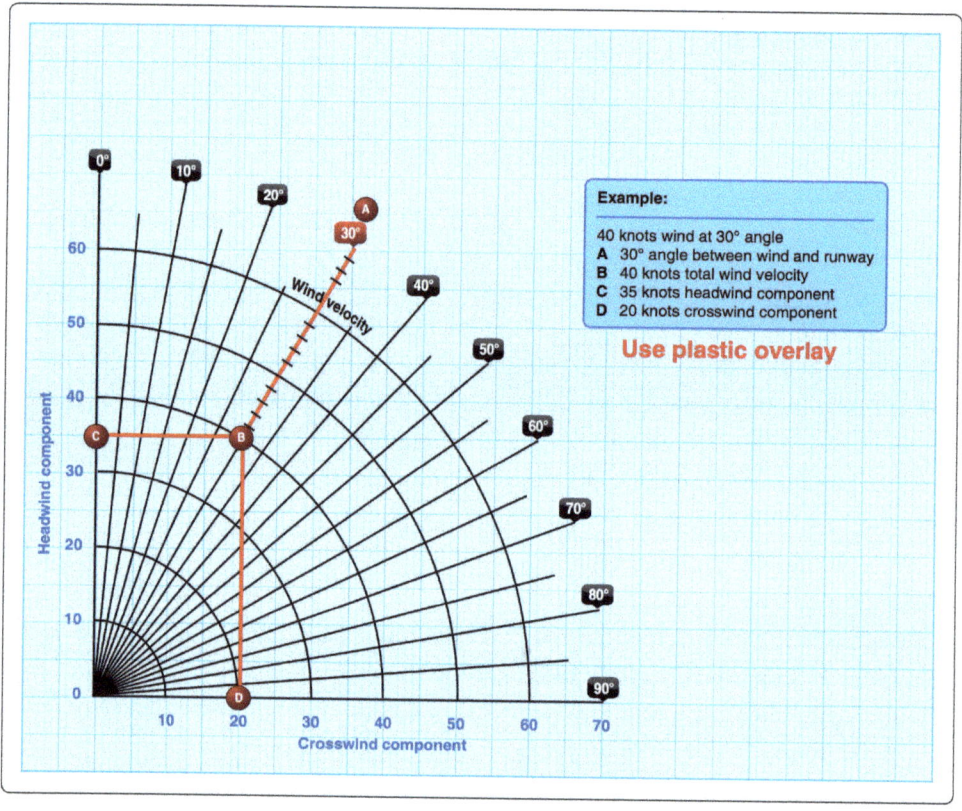

Figure 4.2. Crosswind Component Graph. (Source: FAA-CT-8080-2H, Figure 36)

Let's use the chart to solve a common problem.

Scenario: You are planning to take off down a runway. The wind is reported at **40 knots** coming from a **30-degree angle** to your runway. Your drone's manual says its maximum crosswind component is 25 knots. Can you safely take off?

1. **Find the Wind Angle:** Locate the curved line labeled **30°**.

2. **Find the Wind Velocity:** Find the arc (curved line) representing the **40-knot** wind speed.

3. **Find the Intersection:** Follow the 30° angle line until it intersects with the 40-knot wind speed arc.

4. **Find the Crosswind:** From that intersection point, trace a line straight down to the bottom axis. You will land on **20**. This means you have a **20-knot crosswind component.**

5. **Find the Headwind:** Now, go back to the intersection point and trace a line straight to the left axis. You will land on approximately **35**. This means you have a **35-knot headwind component.**

Conclusion: Since the calculated **20-knot crosswind** is less than your drone's 25-knot maximum, it is safe to proceed with the flight.

Being a great pilot means knowing not just the rules, but also the limits of your machine. By understanding your drone's performance, you can plan smarter, fly safer, and always be in control.

Key Takeaways

- The **Pilot's Operating Handbook (POH)** or flight manual is the best source for your drone's specific performance limitations.

- The four key factors affecting performance are weather, weight, density altitude, and load factor.

- **Load factor** is the stress on the aircraft, which increases significantly during turns.

Likely Test Questions

1. Where can a remote pilot find the official performance limitations for their drone?

2. How does an increase in weight affect drone performance?

3. What is load factor, and when does it increase?

Weight and Balance

Weight and Balance for Your Drone

Hey there, Red Raven pilot! You've learned the rules, you know how to read the sky map, and you can spot bad weather from a mile away. Now, let's talk about something that might seem a bit nerdy, but is super important for a smooth and safe flight: **weight and balance**.

Think of your drone like a finely tuned athlete. It's designed to perform best at a certain weight and when it's perfectly balanced. If it's too heavy or off-balance, it's going to struggle.

The Magic Number: 55

First, let's remember the golden rule of weight we learned in Chapter 2: your drone must weigh **less than 55 pounds** at takeoff. This includes the drone itself, the batteries, and any payload you've attached, like a fancy camera or a specialized sensor. For most of you, this won't be an issue, but if you start flying bigger rigs for professional cinematography or surveying, you'll need to keep this number in mind.

What's a Center of Gravity (CG)?

Now for the "balance" part of "weight and balance." Every aircraft, from a tiny toy drone to a massive jumbo jet, has a **Center of Gravity**, or CG.

Imagine balancing a pencil on your finger. That sweet spot where it balances perfectly is its center of gravity. Your drone has one too. It's the point where the drone's weight is perfectly balanced in all directions.

The drone's manufacturer calculates the correct CG for you. When the CG is in the right spot, your drone is stable, responsive, and flies efficiently.

Don't Upset the Balance!

When you start adding things to your drone—like a new gimbal, a bigger battery, or a package for delivery—you change its weight and can shift its center of gravity.

- **If the CG is too far forward:** The drone will want to pitch down. It will feel "nose-heavy" and might be difficult to fly, especially at low speeds.

- **If the CG is too far back:** The drone will want to pitch up. This can be very dangerous, as it could lead to the drone stalling and falling out of the sky. It will feel "tail-heavy" and unstable.

An out-of-balance drone is an unhappy drone. It has to work much harder to stay stable, which drains the battery faster and puts extra strain on the motors. In the worst-case scenario, it can become uncontrollable and crash.

How to Stay Balanced

So how do you make sure your drone is ready for a safe flight?

1. **Read the Manual:** Your drone's manufacturer will provide all the information you need about its weight limits and how to properly attach payloads. The Pilot's Operating Handbook (POH) or flight manual is your best friend!

2. **Weigh Your Gear:** If you're adding a new payload, weigh it! Make sure your total takeoff weight is under 55 lbs.

3. **Check Your Balance:** After attaching any new gear, check how it affects your drone's balance. Does it feel noticeably nose-heavy or tail-heavy? Follow the manufacturer's instructions for mounting equipment to maintain the proper CG.

Learning from the Pros

On the Part 107 exam, the FAA will test your understanding of these principles using charts from manned aviation. While you won't be putting passengers in your drone, the math (Weight×Arm=Moment) is exactly the same. Let's walk through an example using an official FAA chart in **Figure 5.1**.

Scenario: A pilot weighs 200 lbs, a passenger weighs 150 lbs, and there are 44 gallons of fuel on board. Is the aircraft within its weight and CG limits?

1. **Calculate the Weights:**

   - Empty Weight: 2,015 lbs

   - Pilot (Front Seat): 200 lbs

   - Passenger (Rear Seat): 150 lbs

   - Fuel (44 gal): 264 lbs

   - **Total Weight:** 2,015 + 200 + 150 + 264 = **2,629 lbs**

2. **Calculate the Moments (Moment/100):**

   - Empty Moment: 1,554

   - Pilot (Front): 170

   - Passenger (Rear): 182

   - Fuel (Main Tanks): 198

   - **Total Moment:** 1,554 + 170 + 182 + 198 = **2,104**

3. **Find the Center of Gravity:**

   - CG = (Total Moment × 100) / Total Weight

   - CG = (2,104 × 100) / 2,629 = **79.9 inches**

4. **Check the Limits:** The bottom table shows that for a weight of 2,625 lbs (the closest value), the CG must be between 78.7 and 85.7 inches. Since our calculated CG of 79.9 is within that range, the aircraft is safe to fly.

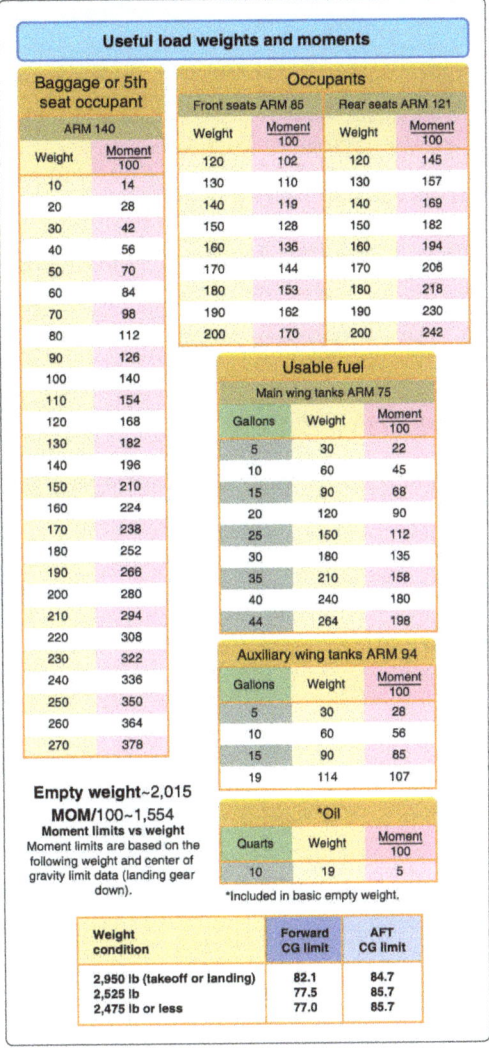

Useful load weights and moments					
Baggage or 5th seat occupant		**Occupants**			
ARM 140		Front seats ARM 85		Rear seats ARM 121	
Weight	Moment/100	Weight	Moment/100	Weight	Moment/100
10	14	120	102	120	145
20	28	130	110	130	157
30	42	140	119	140	169
40	56	150	128	150	182
50	70	160	136	160	194
60	84	170	144	170	206
70	98	180	153	180	218
80	112	190	162	190	230
90	126	200	170	200	242
100	140				
110	154				
120	168				
130	182				
140	196				
150	210				
160	224				
170	238				
180	252				
190	266				
200	280				
210	294				
220	308				
230	322				
240	336				
250	350				
260	364				
270	378				

Usable fuel		
Main wing tanks ARM 75		
Gallons	Weight	Moment/100
5	30	22
10	60	45
15	90	68
20	120	90
25	150	112
30	180	135
35	210	158
40	240	180
44	264	198

Auxiliary wing tanks ARM 94		
Gallons	Weight	Moment/100
5	30	28
10	60	56
15	90	85
19	114	107

Empty weight~2,015
MOM/100~1,554
Moment limits vs weight
Moment limits are based on the following weight and center of gravity limit data (landing gear down).

*Oil		
Quarts	Weight	Moment/100
10	19	5

*Included in basic empty weight.

Weight condition	Forward CG limit	AFT CG limit
2,950 lb (takeoff or landing)	82.1	84.7
2,525 lb	77.5	85.7
2,475 lb or less	77.0	85.7

Figure 5.1. Airplane Weight and Balance Tables. (Source: FAA-CT-8080-2H, Figure 32)

Key Takeaways

- The drone's total weight, including all payloads, must be **less than 55 lbs** at takeoff.

- The **Center of Gravity (CG)** is the point where the drone is perfectly balanced; keeping it within the manufacturer's limits is critical for stability.

- The formula for calculating moment is **Weight × Arm = Moment.**

- An out-of-balance drone is inefficient, unstable, and unsafe.

Likely Test Questions

1. What is the Center of Gravity (CG)?

2. What effect could an out-of-balance drone have on performance?

3. If the CG is shifted too far aft (back), what is the likely result?

Maintenance and Inspections

Pre-Flight Check

You know the rules, the risks, and the environment. Now for the last, and arguably one of the most important, steps you must take before every single flight: **the pre-flight inspection.**

Think of it like a pilot doing a walk-around of their airplane. You would never want a pilot to just jump in and take off without checking the wings and tires, right? Your drone deserves that same level of care. A thorough pre-flight check can be the one thing that catches a small problem before it becomes a big one in the air.

Your Pre-Flight Ritual

You should develop a consistent, systematic routine that you follow before every flight. This ensures you never miss a step. While your drone's manual will have a specific checklist, here are the core things you should always look for.

1. The Drone Itself

- **Frame:** Look at the body and arms of the drone. Are there any cracks or signs of stress?

- **Propellers:** This is a big one. Inspect each propeller for any nicks, cracks, or chips. Even a tiny bit of damage can throw off the balance and lead to vibrations or even failure. If you see damage, **replace it**. Propellers are cheap; drones are not.

- **Motors:** Gently spin each motor by hand. Do they spin freely? Do you feel any grit or resistance?

- **Gimbal and Camera:** Check that the gimbal moves freely and that the camera lens is clean.

- **Screws and Fasteners:** Quickly check to make sure all visible screws are snug.

2. The Brains and Power

- **Batteries:** Are they fully charged? Look for any signs of swelling, puffiness, or damage to the casing. A puffy battery is a dangerous battery and should be safely discharged and disposed of, not used.

- **Controller:** Is your flight controller fully charged?

- **Firmware:** Check for any firmware updates for your drone, controller, and batteries. It's best to do these at home with a good internet connection, not in the field right before a job.

A Note on LiPo Battery Safety

The Lithium Polymer (LiPo) batteries that power your drone are marvels of engineering, packing a huge amount of power into a small package. As the PIC, treating them with respect is one of your most important safety responsibilities. Always follow these best practices for handling your batteries:

Charge with Care: Never leave batteries to charge unattended, especially overnight. It's best practice to be in the same room where you can periodically check on them. Always use the specific charger designed for your batteries to prevent damage.

Store Smart: Treat your batteries like any other piece of valuable electronics. Store them at room temperature inside a fire-resistant LiPo bag or container. Never leave them in a hot car, which can cause permanent damage. For long-term storage (more than a few days), aim to keep them at about a 50% charge, not full.

Handle with Care: Never use a battery that is swollen ("puffy"), dented, punctured, or has a damaged wrapper. If you find a damaged battery, don't use it. Follow local regulations for safely discharging and disposing of it.

Proper battery management is a hallmark of a professional pilot. Taking these simple steps will protect your equipment, ensure your safety, and keep you flying for years to come.

3. The Flight Environment

- **Takeoff and Landing Zone:** Is your chosen spot clear of people, animals, and obstacles? Is the ground level?

- **Weather Check:** Do one last check of the wind and weather conditions. Has anything changed since you checked at home?

Don't Forget the Paperwork!

Part of your pre-flight is making sure you have all your documentation ready. This includes:

- Your Remote Pilot Certificate.

- Your drone's **registration** information.

- Any waivers or airspace authorizations required for the flight.

Post-Flight Love

The work isn't over when the drone lands. After every flight, do a quick post-flight check. Clean the drone, check for any new damage, and charge your batteries so you're ready for the next adventure. Log your flight time in a logbook—this is a great way to track your experience and your drone's maintenance schedule.

Following a strict inspection routine is the mark of a true professional. It shows respect for your equipment and a commitment to safety that will set you apart.

Thinking Ahead: Scheduled Maintenance

Beyond the daily pre-flight and post-flight checks, a professional pilot also follows a scheduled maintenance program. This means tracking the drone's flight hours and performing preventative maintenance to replace parts *before* they fail.

Your drone's manufacturer will provide a recommended maintenance schedule in the manual, which might include tasks like:

- **Replacing propellers** after a certain number of flight hours, even if they don't look damaged.

- **Inspecting and cleaning motors** to ensure they are free of debris.

- **Retiring batteries** after a specific number of charge cycles to prevent unexpected failures in the air.

Keeping a detailed logbook is the best way to track your flight hours and manage your maintenance schedule. This proactive approach is a key part of ensuring the long-term safety and reliability of your drone.

Key Takeaways

- Develop and follow a consistent pre-flight inspection routine before every flight.

- The most critical components to inspect are the **propellers** (for nicks and cracks) and the **batteries** (for swelling or damage).

- Always ensure your **paperwork** (Remote Pilot Certificate, drone registration, authorizations) is accessible during a flight.

Likely Test Questions

1. What is one of the most important items to check during a pre-flight inspection?

2. What physical characteristic is a sign of a damaged or unsafe LiPo battery?

3. What three documents should a remote pilot have with them during a flight operation?

Fit to Fly

Your Health and Being a Pilot

We've spent a lot of time talking about your drone's health—its weight, its balance, its performance. But now it's time to talk about the most critical component of any safe flight: **the pilot.** That's you.

Being "fit to fly" isn't about being able to run a marathon. It's about being in the right condition—physically and mentally—to safely operate your drone. As the Pilot in Command, you have a responsibility to make sure you are 100% ready for every single flight.

The "IMSAFE" Checklist

Pilots of all types use a simple mnemonic to do a quick personal health check before they fly. It's called **"IMSAFE,"** and it's a fantastic habit to get into. IMSAFE stands for Illness, Medication, Stress, Alcohol, Fatigue, and Emotion/Eating.

Before every flight, do a personal health check using these official items.

1. **I**llness: Do you have any symptoms of being sick? A headache, a stuffy nose, or an upset stomach can be incredibly distracting and can seriously impact your ability to focus.

2. **M**edication: Are you taking any medication? Do not fly while using any medication, prescription or over-the-counter, that could affect your mental or physical abilities. Pay special attention to common **antihistamines** (for allergies) and cold remedies, as they are known to cause drowsiness. If you are unsure, consult an Aviation Medical Examiner (AME).

3. **S**tress: Are you feeling stressed out? Maybe you had a tough day at work or a fight with a family member. Stress distracts us and can lead to poor decision-making. If your head isn't in the game, it might be best to leave the drone on the ground.

4. **A**lcohol: This is a hard and fast rule. A remote pilot cannot fly if they have a blood alcohol concentration (BAC) of **0.04% or greater**, or if they have consumed any alcoholic beverage within the preceding **8 hours** (the "8 hours from bottle to throttle" rule). The best policy? Don't mix flying and alcohol. Ever.

5. **F**atigue: Are you tired? Fatigue is a sneaky and dangerous factor in aviation. A lack of sleep can impair your judgment just as much as alcohol can. Make sure you are well-rested before every flight.

6. **E**motion / Eating: Are you emotionally upset? Similar to stress, strong emotions can cloud your judgment. Also, have you eaten properly? Low blood sugar can make you feel weak or dizzy, which is the last thing you want when you're in command of an aircraft.

Physiological Factors (Vision & Illusions)

Your Most Important Sensors: Your Eyes

As a remote pilot, you rely almost entirely on your vision for situational awareness. The FAA expects you to understand how your eyes work, especially at night.

1. **Rods and Cones:** Your eyes have two types of cells. **Cones** are in the center of your vision and detect color and detail in bright light. **Rods** are in your peripheral vision and are responsible for detecting movement and seeing in low light, but they don't see color well.

2. **Night Scanning:** At night, looking directly at an object (like another aircraft) is less effective because it uses your cones. Instead, use a **scanning technique**, looking slightly *off-center* from where you want to see. This uses your rods, which are more sensitive to light, and makes it easier to spot faint lights or movement. It takes about **30 minutes** for your eyes to fully adapt to darkness.

3. **Visual Illusions:** Your brain can be tricked, especially at night. Be aware of illusions like a **false horizon**, where you might mistake a line of city lights or clouds for the actual horizon, or **autokinesis**, where a single, stationary light can appear to be moving if you stare at it for too long. Always trust your drone's instruments and maintain a clear sense of your location.

Hazardous Attitudes (And Their Antidotes!)

Sometimes, it's our own attitude that can be the biggest threat to safety. The FAA has identified five "hazardous attitudes" that can get pilots into trouble as shown in **Figure 7.1**. See if you recognize any of these in yourself.

Being a safe pilot starts with an honest self-assessment before every flight. Using the IMSAFE checklist and keeping hazardous attitudes in check will ensure that the person in command is just as ready as the aircraft they're flying. Here's what the FAA would like you to know:

The Five Hazardous Attitudes	Antidote
Anti-authority: "Don't tell me." This attitude is found in people who do not like anyone telling them what to do. In a sense, they are saying, "No one can tell me what to do." They may be resentful of having someone tell them what to do or may regard rules, regulations, and procedures as silly or unnecessary. However, it is always your prerogative to question authority if you feel it is in error.	Follow the rules. They are usually right.
Impulsivity: "Do it quickly." This is the attitude of people who frequently feel the need to do something, anything, immediately. They do not stop to think about what they are about to do, they do not select the best alternative, and they do the first thing that comes to mind.	Not so fast. Think first.
Invulnerability: "It won't happen to me." Many people falsely believe that accidents happen to others, but never to them. They know accidents can happen, and they know that anyone can be affected. However, they never really feel or believe that they will be personally involved. Pilots who think this way are more likely to take chances and increase risk.	It could happen to me.
Macho: "I can do it." Pilots who are always trying to prove that they are better than anyone else think, "I can do it—I'll show them." Pilots with this type of attitude will try to prove themselves by taking risks in order to impress others. While this pattern is thought to be a male characteristic, women are equally susceptible.	Taking chances is foolish.
Resignation: "What's the use?" Pilots who think, "What's the use?" do not see themselves as being able to make a great deal of difference in what happens to them. When things go well, the pilot is apt to think that it is good luck. When things go badly, the pilot may feel that someone is out to get them or attribute it to bad luck. The pilot will leave the action to others, for better or worse. Sometimes, such pilots will even go along with unreasonable requests just to be a "nice guy."	I'm not helpless. I can make a difference.

Figure 7.1. The five hazardous attitudes identified through past and contemporary study. (FAA-G-8082-22), Figure 10.2)

Key Takeaways

1. Use the **IMSAFE** checklist (Illness, Medication, Stress, Alcohol, Fatigue, Emotion/Eating) to perform a personal health assessment before every flight.

2. Recognize and counteract the **Five Hazardous Attitudes**: Anti-Authority, Impulsivity, Invulnerability, Macho, and Resignation.

3. The FAA has a strict "8 hours from bottle to throttle" rule regarding alcohol.

Likely Test Questions

1. What does the 'S' in the IMSAFE checklist stand for?

2. A pilot who thinks "accidents only happen to other people" is displaying which hazardous attitude?

3. What is the FAA's rule regarding alcohol consumption before a flight?

Aeronautical Decision-Making

Making the Right Call: Aeronautical Decision-Making

So far, you've learned the rules, the environment your drone flies in, and how to make sure both you and your drone are in top shape. Now, let's tie it all together. This chapter is about **Aeronautical Decision-Making (ADM)**.

That sounds complicated, but it's not. ADM is simply the art of making good, safe decisions before and during your flight. It's a systematic way of thinking that helps you see problems coming and deal with them before they become emergencies.

Managing Risk Like a Pro

A huge part of ADM is **risk management**. Every single flight has some level of risk. The wind could pick up, a dog could run into your landing zone, or your battery could drain faster than you expected. A professional pilot doesn't ignore these risks; they manage them.

The process is simple:

- **Identify Hazards:** What could possibly go wrong?

- **Assess the Risk:** How likely is it to happen, and how bad would it be if it did?

- **Mitigate the Risk:** What can I do to make it safer?

The PAVE Checklist: Your Go-To Tool for Spotting Trouble

How do you spot potential problems? A great way is to use the **PAVE** checklist. It helps you scan the four key areas of any flight.

- **P**ilot-in-Command: Are you truly fit to fly? Go back to that IMSAFE checklist. Are you tired, stressed, or sick?

  - *Hazard:* You only got four hours of sleep last night.

  - *Mitigation:* Postpone the flight. A tired pilot makes bad decisions.

- **A**ircraft: Is your drone ready? Is the battery fully charged? Is the firmware updated? Did you do a pre-flight check of the propellers and frame?

    - *Hazard:* You noticed a small crack in one of the propellers.

    - *Mitigation:* Don't fly! Replace the propeller immediately. A broken prop in mid-air is a guaranteed crash.

- en**V**ironment: What's the world like today? Check the weather, the airspace, and any obstacles like trees or power lines. Are there people or animals nearby?

    - *Hazard:* The forecast calls for gusty winds later in the afternoon.

    - *Mitigation:* Plan to fly in the morning to avoid the worst of the wind.

- **E**xternal Pressures: Is something making you feel rushed? Do you have a client looking over your shoulder? Are you trying to get that "one epic shot" for social media?

    - *Hazard:* A client is pressuring you to fly a little closer to a building than you're comfortable with.

    - *Mitigation:* Be firm and professional. Explain the safety risks and the regulations. It's better to lose a shot than to lose your drone or your license.

The 3P Model: Your In-Flight Decision Loop

Okay, so PAVE is great for planning, but what about when you're in the air? For that, you can use the **3P Model: Perceive, Process, Perform.** It's a continuous loop of good decision-making.

1. **Perceive:** Notice a change in the situation. (e.g., "I see a flock of seagulls gathering near my drone.")

2. **Process:** Think about what that change means for your flight. (e.g., "A bird strike could damage my drone and cause it to crash. This is a serious hazard.")

3. **Perform:** Take action to fix it. (e.g., "I am descending to a lower altitude and flying away from the birds to land safely.")

Good Aeronautical Decision-Making isn't a skill you learn overnight. It's a habit you build over time. By using tools like PAVE and the 3P model on every single flight, you'll develop the judgment and confidence of a true professional pilot.

Putting It All Together: Your Pre-Flight Workflow

Good Aeronautical Decision-Making isn't just a thought process; it's a series of concrete actions you take before every flight. The FAA legally requires these actions under regulation. This workflow combines that rule with the risk management principles you've learned.

As the **Remote Pilot in Command (RPIC)**, you are directly responsible for and the final authority over the entire operation. This pre-flight check is your duty:

Step 1: Assess the Operating Environment

Before you even power on the drone, assess the "V" (enVironment) from your PAVE checklist.

- **Weather:** Check the latest METARs, TAFs, and forecasts. Are the winds, visibility, and temperatures within safe limits for you and your drone?

- **Airspace & Restrictions:** Is the airspace controlled? Do you need LAANC authorization? Check for any Temporary Flight Restrictions (TFRs) or Notices to Air Missions (NOTAMs) at 1800wxbrief.com.

- **Ground Hazards:** Identify potential risks on the surface, including people, vehicles, buildings, and obstacles like wires or trees.

Step 2: Inspect the Aircraft and Systems

Next, ensure your aircraft is in a condition for safe operation (§107.15). This is the "A" from your PAVE checklist.

- **Physical Check:** Inspect the propellers, frame, and motors for any damage.

- **Power:** Ensure all flight batteries are charged and physically sound (no swelling or damage).

- **Payload:** Verify that any cameras or other attachments are secured and don't negatively affect the drone's balance or flight characteristics.

- **Control Links:** Power on the controller and drone to confirm a strong, working link between them.

- **Remote ID:** Verify that your drone's Remote ID system is active and broadcasting.

Step 3: Brief All Participants

Even if your crew is just you and a Visual Observer, a pre-flight briefing is mandatory. This covers the "P" (Pilot/People) from PAVE.

- **Operating Conditions:** Discuss the flight plan, altitudes, and objectives.

- **Emergency Procedures:** What is the plan for a lost link, low battery, or manned aircraft encounter?

- **Roles and Responsibilities:** Clearly state who is the RPIC, who is the VO, and what each person's duties are.

- **Potential Hazards:** Talk about the specific risks you identified in Step 1.

Key Takeaways

- Use the **PAVE** checklist (Pilot, Aircraft, enVironment, External pressures) to identify potential hazards before a flight.

- Use the **3P Model** (Perceive, Process, Perform) as a continuous loop for making good decisions during a flight.

- Effective risk management involves **identifying, assessing, and mitigating** hazards.

Likely Test Questions

1. What do the letters in the PAVE checklist stand for?

2. A client pressuring you to fly in unsafe conditions is an example of which element of the PAVE checklist?

3. Describe the three steps of the 3P model for in-flight decision-making.

Mayday! Mayday!

Handling Emergencies Like a Pro

Okay, let's talk about something that we hope you never have to use, but absolutely need to be ready for: emergencies. It's easy to think, "it won't happen to me," but even the best pilots can face unexpected challenges. The difference between a close call and a catastrophe is being prepared.

The good news is that with a cool head and a clear plan, you can handle most in-flight issues like a seasoned pro. This chapter is all about giving you that plan.

The Most Common Curveballs

While a drone emergency can take many forms, most issues fall into a few common categories. Here's what you're most likely to encounter:

- **Lost Link and Flyaways:** This is when your controller loses its connection to the drone. Your drone is suddenly on its own! Most modern drones have a pre-set plan for this, like automatically returning to its takeoff spot (Return-to-Home or RTH). **Know your drone's lost link procedure before you ever take off!**

- **Critically Low Battery:** You get so caught up in getting the perfect shot that you forget to check your battery level. Suddenly, your controller is screaming at you with a low battery warning. This is a classic emergency that is almost always preventable with good planning.

- **Sudden Weather Tantrums:** The forecast was clear, but a sudden, powerful gust of wind appears out of nowhere, or a surprise rain shower pops up.

- **System Malfunctions:** You get a scary warning message on your screen, like "motor error" or "compass failure." Or worse, you **physically see a propeller stop spinning.**

- **Unexpected Visitors:** A low-flying airplane or helicopter appears on the horizon, or a curious dog (or person!) wanders right under your drone.

It is the **Remote Pilot in Command's responsibility** to know what their drone will do in a lost link situation. Most drones, like those from DJI, default to a "Return-to-Home" (RTH) sequence, but you must ensure the RTH altitude is set correctly for your specific flight area to clear any obstacles on the way back. Never assume the default settings are safe for your operation.

Your Three-Step Emergency Plan: Fly, Assess, Act

When something goes wrong, it's easy to panic. The key is to have a simple, go-to action plan. For pilots of all kinds, it boils down to this:

1. **Fly the Drone First.** This is your absolute number one priority. Before you try to figure out *what* went wrong, make sure you are still in control of the aircraft. Is it drifting? Is it stable? Use your controls to keep it steady and in a safe position.

2. **Assess the Situation.** Once the drone is stable, take a deep breath and quickly figure out what's happening. What are the warnings on your screen? What do you see and hear? Is the drone making a weird noise? How much battery do you have left? Where is the safest place to land?

3. **Act Deliberately.** Now, execute your plan. Don't just react—act with purpose. This usually means one thing: **Land as soon as safely possible.** This might mean initiating your drone's Return-to-Home function or manually flying it to a pre-planned emergency landing spot.

While the Three-Step emergency plan is what the FAA would like you to know for the test. The goal is always to avoid harm to people, property and land the drone safely as quickly as you can.

While these are not on the exam, it's very important that you know these as a remote pilot. This will give you an action plan in case any of these scenarios come up.

Here's what to actually do in an Emergency

EMERGENCY	HOW TO SPOT IT	POSSIBLE CAUSES	WHAT TO DO
Low Battery	App warnings ("Low," "Critical"), rapid percentage drop.	Poor flight planning, high winds, cold weather, old battery.	Turn directly home, descend to a lower altitude, and land with a power reserve.
Lost GPS (ATTI Mode)	"GPS signal weak" warnings, the drone drifts with the wind.	Flying in "urban canyons," satellite obstruction, equipment failure.	Fly gentle, smooth inputs. Point the drone's nose toward home and avoid hard stops.
Compass Error	"Compass error" warnings, "toilet-bowl" drifting, sudden yawing.	Magnetic interference (rebar, power lines), improper calibration.	Climb slightly for safety, then fly away from the interference source.
Lost Control Link	"RC signal lost" warning, sticks are unresponsive.	Flying behind obstacles, exceeding range, antenna misorientation.	Let the failsafe (RTH) work. Be ready to take back control if the signal returns.
Lost Video Link	Camera feed is black or laggy, but controls still work.	Exceeding range, antenna issues, RF interference, loose cable.	Hold position. Use your Visual Observer (VO) or your own eyes to fly back. Use RTH if needed.
High Winds / Gusts	The drone struggles to fly into the wind, visible dust or thrashing trees.	Inaccurate forecast, unpredictable gust front from a storm.	Descend to a lower altitude where winds are lighter. Land immediately if a gust front approaches.

EMERGENCY	HOW TO SPOT IT	POSSIBLE CAUSES	WHAT TO DO
Turbulence / Shear	Sudden, sharp jolts in altitude or attitude near obstacles.	Flying on the downwind side of buildings, hills, or trees.	Move upwind (into the wind) to find smoother air. Avoid flying on the downwind side of obstacles.
Geofence Restriction	App warnings ("Restricted Zone"), drone refuses to enter an area or auto-lands.	Lack of pre-flight planning, flying near a sensitive location.	Do not fight the automation. Steer the drone to a clear spot on the ground during an auto-land.
People in Area	A person or vehicle enters your pre-flight safety zone.	Inadequate ground setup, bystanders ignoring warnings.	Climb straight up or move away to create distance. Land or hold position until the area is clear.
Manned Aircraft	You see or hear a plane or helicopter nearby.	Failure to check for local traffic (e.g., hospital helipads).	Immediately descend and move away from its flight path. Land if necessary. Yielding is mandatory.
Bird Harassment	Birds are circling, diving at, or mobbing the drone.	Flying near a nest or feeding area, territorial birds (raptors).	Descend and fly away from the birds' territory quickly. Do not act aggressively toward them.
Rain / Moisture	Raindrops appear on the camera lens, or you get humidity warnings.	Un-forecasted rain, flying in high humidity or fog.	Land at the closest safe landing zone immediately to prevent water damage.
Motor / Prop Failure	Sudden vibrations, error messages, or uncommanded yaw/roll.	Pre-existing prop damage, object strike, component burnout.	If controllable, land immediately. If control is lost, perform a controlled crash away from people.

EMERGENCY	HOW TO SPOT IT	POSSIBLE CAUSES	WHAT TO DO
Flyaway	The drone ignores all commands and flies off in a direction.	Severe compass error, GPS spoofing, major hardware failure.	Switch flight modes (e.g., GPS to ATTI) if possible to regain control. Cancel RTH if it's flying into a hazard.
Battery Fire / Smoke	The battery is swelling, you smell smoke, or the app shows a thermal warning.	Using a damaged/puffed battery, internal short circuit.	Land immediately in a clear, non-ammable area (e.g., dirt or concrete). Keep a safe distance.
Lost VLOS	You can no longer see the drone with your own eyes.	Pilot distraction, sun glare, flying too far away, background camouflage.	Stop and hover. Use your VO to re-acquire sight. If you cannot, initiate RTH.
Obstruction Entanglement	The drone is stuck in a tree, on a wire, or on a building.	Poor situational awareness, unexpected wind gust.	Disarm the motors immediately to prevent further damage. Plan a safe physical recovery.

The Not-So-Fun Paperwork: Reporting an Accident

Sometimes, even with the best planning, accidents happen. Despite careful preflight checks, weather briefings, and airspace reviews, unforeseen circumstances can still arise – a sudden gust of wind, an unexpected bird strike, or a momentary loss of signal. Human error, equipment malfunction, or environmental factors can all contribute to an incident. The point isn't to assume the worst will happen, but to acknowledge that no flight is ever risk-free and that being ready to respond is part of being a responsible pilot.

You must report an accident to the FAA within 10 days if it results in:

1. **Serious injury to any person.**

2. **Loss of consciousness.**

3. **Damage to any property, other than the drone itself, costing more than $500 to repair or replace.**

You can file a report via the FAA DroneZone website under Part 107 Accident Reporting. You don't need to report a flight if you just scratch up your drone's landing gear. But if you crash into someone's roof and cause $1,000 in damage, you'll need to file a report.

What to Capture Now (Accident Checklist):

1. **Who was involved** (injured parties, property owner, witnesses).

2. **What happened** (type of accident, damage caused).

3. **Where it happened** (address, GPS coordinates if possible).

4. **When it happened** (exact time/date).

5. **Contacts & Photos** - Exchange names/numbers and take clear photos of the scene and damage.

Being prepared for an emergency isn't about being paranoid; it's about being a professional. Knowing these steps will give you the confidence to handle whatever the sky throws at you.

Key Takeaways

- In any emergency, follow the three-step plan: Fly the aircraft, Assess the situation, Act deliberately.

- Know your drone's **lost link procedure** (e.g., Return-to-Home) before you take off.

- You must report an accident to the FAA within 10 days if it causes **serious injury** or property damage **exceeding $500** (to repair or replace).

Likely Test Questions

1. What is the first action a remote pilot should take in an in-flight emergency?

2. Under what circumstances must an accident be reported to the FAA?

3. What is the most common procedure for a drone that has lost its connection to the controller?

Crew Resource Management

Teamwork Makes the Dream Work

When you hear the term "flight crew," you probably picture airline pilots in a complex cockpit, talking over headsets. But guess what? Even as a drone pilot, you're part of a crew—even if that crew is just you!

This chapter is about **Crew Resource Management**, or **CRM**. It's a fancy term for a simple idea: using all available resources (people, equipment, and information) to conduct a safe and efficient flight. Let's break down what that means for you.

Who's on Your Drone Team?

A drone operation isn't always a solo act. You might have a team working with you, and it's important that everyone knows their role.

- **The Remote Pilot in Command (PIC):** That's you, the licensed pilot! You are the captain of the ship. You're responsible for the entire operation, from pre-flight checks to the final landing.

- **The Person Manipulating the Controls:** This is the person who is actually flying the drone. It might be you, or it could be someone else flying under your direct supervision. But remember, as the PIC, you're still in charge.

- **The Visual Observer (VO):** This is your trusted teammate, your second set of eyes. Their one and only job during the flight is to watch the drone and the surrounding airspace. A VO helps you meet the FAA's requirement to maintain visual line-of-sight (VLOS), but only if there is continuous, immediate communication with you, the Remote Pilot in Command. The VO must be able to alert you instantly about hazards—such as birds, other aircraft, or people approaching—so that you can perform your required "see and avoid" duties under Part 107.

The Secrets of Good Teamwork

Good CRM boils down to a few key principles, whether you have a team of three or you're flying solo.

- **Clear Communication:** Before the flight, hold a briefing. Talk about the mission, the flight path, potential hazards, and what to do in an emergency. During the flight, use simple, clear, and direct language. Instead of "it's over there," say "bird, 3 o'clock high."

- **Situational Awareness:** This means knowing what's going on around you at all times. As the pilot, you might be focused on the camera feed. Your Visual Observer is your secret weapon for situational awareness, watching the drone itself and the sky around it.

- **Speaking Up:** This is huge. Everyone on the team has a responsibility to speak up if they see a problem. As the PIC, you need to create an environment where your VO feels comfortable saying, "Hey, that plane looks a little too close," or "I think you're drifting toward those trees." A good PIC listens to their crew.

Being a Crew of One

Flying solo? You still need to practice good CRM. You just have to be your own PIC, pilot, and VO. This means:

- **Avoid Distractions:** Don't text, answer phone calls, or let yourself get distracted from flying safely.

- **Manage Your Tasks:** Don't try to do too much at once. If you need to change a complex camera setting, it might be best to bring the drone to a stable hover first.

- **Use Checklists:** A checklist is your best friend when you're flying solo. It ensures you don't forget a critical step in your pre-flight or post-flight routine. We'll talk more about this later!

Whether you're flying with a team or by yourself, thinking about CRM will make you a safer, more professional, and more effective pilot.

Key Takeaways

1. Even when flying solo, you are a "crew" and must manage your resources effectively.

2. The primary role of a **Visual Observer (VO)** is to watch the drone and the surrounding airspace to help maintain safety.

3. Good CRM depends on clear communication, situational awareness, and a willingness for all team members to speak up if they see a hazard.

Likely Test Questions

1. What is Crew Resource Management (CRM)?

2. What is the primary responsibility of a Visual Observer?

3. Why is a pre-flight briefing important for good CRM?

Radio Communication Basics

"Roger That!"

Talking on an aviation radio can seem intimidating. It's full of strange words, numbers, and a special alphabet. But here's the good news: as a drone pilot, your main job is to listen. Monitoring radio chatter is one of the best ways to build a mental picture of what's happening in the sky around you, especially when you're operating near an airport.

This chapter will give you the basics so you can "decode" what you hear – and if needed, make a professional, concise transmission that other pilots will understand instantly.

The Airport Party Line: CTAF

Imagine you're flying near a small, local airport that doesn't have an air traffic control tower. How do pilots know where other planes are? They use a "party line" called the **CTAF**, or **Common Traffic Advisory Frequency**.

Pilots use the CTAF to announce who they are, where they are, and what they intend to do. By monitoring this frequency on an aviation radio, you can hear a pilot announce that they are "10 miles out and inbound for landing," which tells you it's a good time to be extra vigilant or land your drone.

You can find the CTAF frequency for a specific airport on a sectional chart. It's usually marked with a "C" inside a circle next to the name of the airport like the example shown in **Figure 11.1**.

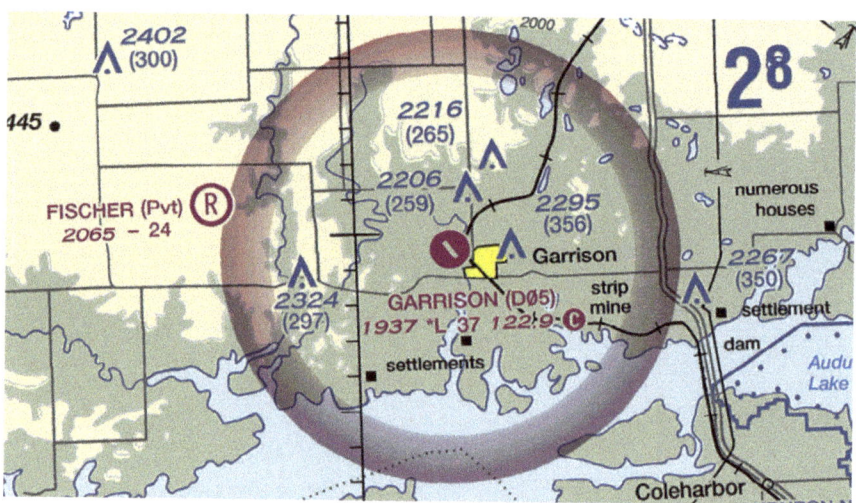

Figure 11.1. Sectional Chart Excerpt (Source: FAA-CT-8080-2H, Figure 21)

The ABCs for Pilots

Have you ever tried to spell something over a loud, crackly phone line? Is it "B" or "D" or "P"? It can be tough to hear the difference. That's why pilots use the **Phonetic Alphabet**. It's a standardized set of words for each letter to make sure there's no confusion.

You absolutely need to know this, both for the exam and for understanding radio calls.

So, an aircraft with the tail number "N357BD" would identify itself as "**November Three Five Seven Bravo Delta.**"

The Phonetic Alphabet

LETTER	WORD	LETTER	WORD
A	Alpha	N	November
B	Bravo	O	Oscar
C	Charlie	P	Papa
D	Delta	Q	Quebec
E	Echo	R	Romeo
F	Foxtrot	S	Sierra
G	Golf	T	Tango
H	Hotel	U	Uniform
I	India	V	Victor
J	Juliett	W	Whiskey
K	Kilo	X	X-ray
L	Lima	Y	Yankee
M	Mike	Z	Zulu

How to Decode a Radio Call

Most standard radio calls follow a simple pattern. When you hear one, listen for these four things:

1. **WHO they're calling:** e.g., "Anysville Traffic..."

2. **WHO they are:** e.g., "...Skyhawk Niner Two One Papa Charlie..."

3. **WHERE they are:** e.g., "...is 5 miles to the east at 3,500 feet..."

4. **WHAT they're doing:** e.g., "...will be entering the pattern for landing."

Just by listening, you now know there's a plane named "921PC" to your east, and it's getting ready to land. That's powerful information!

Should *You* Be Talking?

Part 107 doesn't require drone pilots to make radio calls. However, if you're flying near an airport, it is an incredible safety-enhancing practice. You don't need to say much.

A simple, clear call like this works wonders:

> "Anysville traffic, unmanned aircraft operations, 1 mile northwest of the field, at or below 400 feet, Anysville traffic."

This simple call tells every pilot listening that you're there, making the sky safer for everyone.

Listening to radio chatter is a skill, and it takes practice. But it's one of the best tools you have for situational awareness.

How to Talk the Talk: Sample Radio Calls

Knowing how to listen to the radio is a critical skill, but sometimes you should be the one talking. Making a simple, clear radio call on the CTAF (Common Traffic Advisory Frequency) is one of the most professional things you can do to enhance safety when operating near an airport.

You don't need to have a long conversation. The goal is to make a clear, concise announcement that tells the other pilots in the area who you are, where you are, and what you're doing.

Here is a simple script you can follow. Just fill in the blanks.

The Basic Announcement Script:

"[Airport Name] traffic, [Your Company Name] unmanned aircraft operations, [Location], at or below [Altitude] feet, [Airport Name] traffic."Let's break it down:

- **"[Airport Name] traffic..."**: This is how you start and end every call. You're addressing everyone listening on that airport's frequency.

- **"[Your Company Name] unmanned aircraft operations..."**: This clearly identifies who you are (Red Raven) and what you are (a drone). Using "unmanned aircraft" is the most professional term.

- **"[Location]..."**: Be specific and simple. Use a direction and distance from the airport. For example, "one mile northwest of the field" or "over the high school, two miles east."

- **"...at or below [Altitude] feet."**: Always state your maximum altitude, which will almost always be "at or below 400 feet." This tells airplane pilots that you will be well below their normal traffic pattern altitude.

Keep in mind you should only transmit what helps others see you.

Putting It All Together (Examples):

"Anysville traffic, Red Raven unmanned aircraft operations, two miles east over the power plant, at or below 400 feet, Anysville traffic."

"Smith Field traffic, Red Raven drone operations, one-half mile south of the runway, at or below 200 feet, Smith Field traffic."

Making a radio call might feel intimidating at first, but with a little practice, it will become second nature. It's a simple step that makes the sky safer for everyone.

What if ATC Loses Contact?

If you are operating in controlled airspace under a specific authorization from Air Traffic Control and you lose radio contact, you are expected to follow a standard procedure. Unless you have made a different plan with ATC beforehand, you should land your drone as soon as safely possible. This ensures you do not become an uncommunicative hazard in controlled airspace.

Key Takeaways

- Radio calls on the CTAF should be clear, concise, and follow a standard format.

- The goal is to announce who you are, where you are, and what you are doing.

- Always state your location in relation to the airport and specify that you are operating "at or below 400 feet."

Likely Test Questions

1. What is the proper way to initiate a radio call on a CTAF?

2. You are operating a drone one mile north of Anytown Airport. What would be the most appropriate radio call?

3. Why is it important to state your operating altitude in a radio call?

Navigating the Airport Environment

Airport Savvy

Alright, let's talk about the place where manned aviation and drone operations are most likely to cross paths: **the airport**. Flying near an airport as a drone pilot might sound scary, but it doesn't have to be. By understanding how an airport works and what to look for, you can operate safely and professionally in this busier environment.

Remember from Chapter 3, you **must** have FAA authorization (usually through LAANC) to fly in the controlled airspace around most airports (Classes B, C, and D). This chapter is about what to do once you have that authorization.

The Anatomy of an Airport

Let's quickly go over the main parts of an airport you should know.

Runways: These are the big strips where planes take off and land. They are numbered based on their magnetic direction. For example, a runway pointing east (90 degrees) would be called "Runway 9," while the opposite end pointing west (270 degrees) would be "Runway 27." Staying far away from runway approach and departure paths is critical.

Taxiways: These are the "roads" that planes use to get from the terminal to the runway.

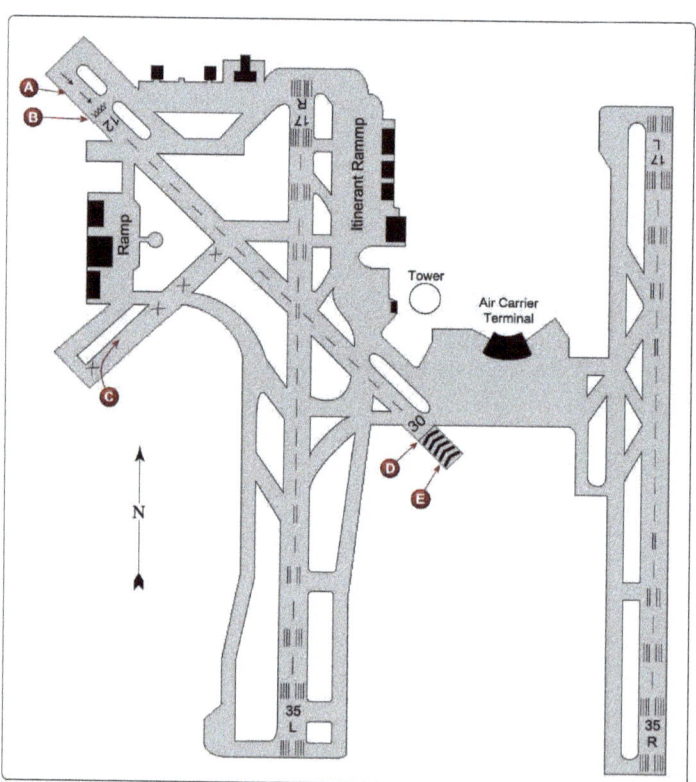

Figure 12.1. Airport Diagram. (Source: FAA-CT-8080-2H, Figure 48)

Traffic Pattern: The Highway in the Sky

Manned aircraft don't just fly randomly around an airport. To keep things safe and organized, they follow a standard "highway in the sky" called a **traffic pattern**. Think of it as an imaginary rectangular road that circles a runway. It's designed to make sure every pilot knows where to expect other aircraft. **Figure 12.2** shows the physical runway in black while the traffic pattern in the sky is in gray.

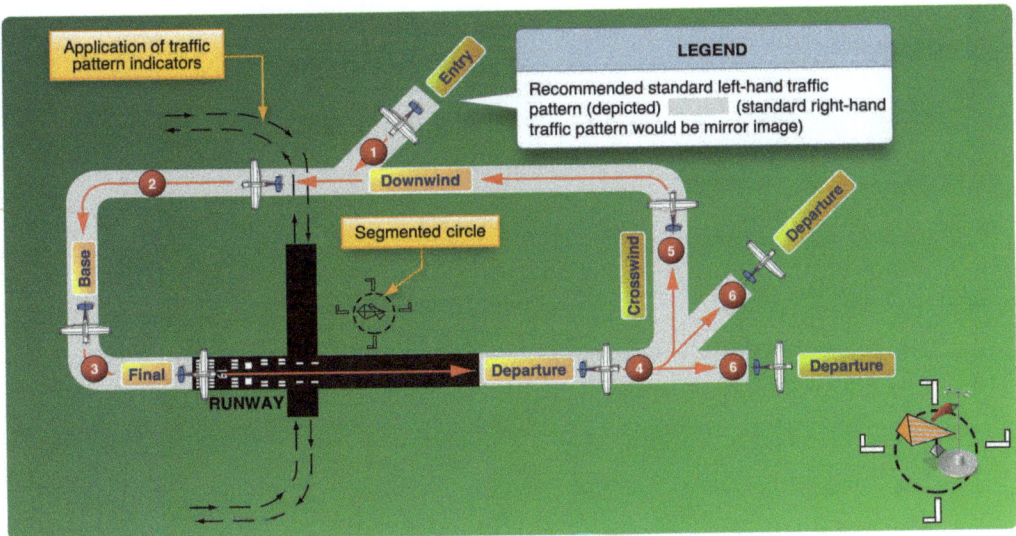

Figure 12.2. Traffic pattern operations—single runway. (Source: FAA-H-8083-25C, Figure 14-39)

As you can see in the diagram, the pattern is made of a few simple legs:

- **Upwind/Departure:** The plane takes off and flies straight out from the runway.

- **Crosswind:** A short turn that connects the departure to the downwind leg.

- **Downwind:** The plane flies parallel to the runway, but in the opposite direction it will land. This is where pilots often make radio calls and run their landing checklists.

- **Base:** A short turn that connects the downwind leg to the final approach.

- **Final:** The plane is lined up with the runway, descending for a landing. This is the most critical phase of the approach.

As a drone pilot, your job isn't to fly this pattern. Your job is to **know it exists**. By understanding this diagram, you can predict where airplanes are most likely to be, which helps you stay aware and, most importantly, stay out of their way. Always be extra cautious when flying near the final approach path of any runway.

Reading the Pavement: A Guide to Airport Markings

Even though you won't taxi an airplane, understanding how **manned aircraft move** on the ground helps you predict where they'll be–and stay out of their way. Pilots follow painted **markings** and **signs** to get from ramp → taxiway → runway and back. Knowing these cues lets a remote pilot anticipate traffic flows near an airport and pick safe launch/landing spots, holding areas, and contingency abort directions.
How pilots "know where to go"

- **Taxiways** are the paved paths aircraft use on the ground. Yellow **centerlines** and **edge markings** keep them on the route.

- **Mandatory/hold short cues** tell pilots where they **must stop** until cleared. They have red signs with painted "bars".

- **Special areas** like the ILS critical area have unique markings so aircraft don't block radio signals when weather is low. They look like a yellow ladder.

- **Vehicle roadways** on ramps are marked so trucks/carts don't mix with aircraft routes. They are marked with with white edges.

Let's break down this typical airport scene in **Figure 12.3** from the FAA's testing materials.

Here's what each letter means and how to interpret it:

A. **Runway Holding Position Sign & Marking (Hold Short of the Runway)**
Red sign with white runway numbers next to the **four-bar hold line** (two solid/two dashed). This is the "**stop here**" point before entering a runway. Pilots may not cross without a clearance at towered fields (or without ensuring it's safe at non-towered fields). As a remote pilot, avoid operating anywhere aircraft will queue at these points.

B. **ILS Critical Area Boundary Marking**
"Ladder-style" yellow markings used to protect the **Instrument Landing System** antennas from interference. When the ILS is active (often in low weather), ATC may hold aircraft at this line. Expect aircraft to pause here; don't hover nearby with a drone.

C. **Vehicle Roadway Markings (Ramp Roadway Edge & Center Lines)**
White solid "edge" stripes (or "zipper" edges) and dashed centerlines define **vehicle lanes** on the ramp so tugs and fuel trucks stay out of aircraft paths. If you're flying near a ramp, remember vehicles may follow these lanes at any time.

D. **Runway Holding Position Marking (Painted Hold Short Bars)**
The **four yellow lines** across the taxiway—**solid** on the side that must hold, **dashed** on the runway side. This is the painted companion to the red sign in **A**. Aircraft stop here for takeoff or when crossing. Remote pilots should stay well clear; this is a runway-incursion hotspot.

E. **Taxiway Holding Position Marking (Taxiway/Taxiway Hold)**
Used at some airports where ATC needs aircraft to **hold short of another taxiway**. Depicted in the supplement's figure set and commonly tested. It tells pilots where to pause before entering or crossing a busy taxiway. Expect momentary queues here as well.

F. **Taxiway Edge (Boundary) Markings**

Double continuous **yellow edge lines** that separate the usable taxiway from pavement not intended for aircraft (shoulder/ramp). They help keep aircraft on the movement area and out of non-movement zones. For drones, treat areas inside the edge lines as high-priority aircraft routes to avoid.

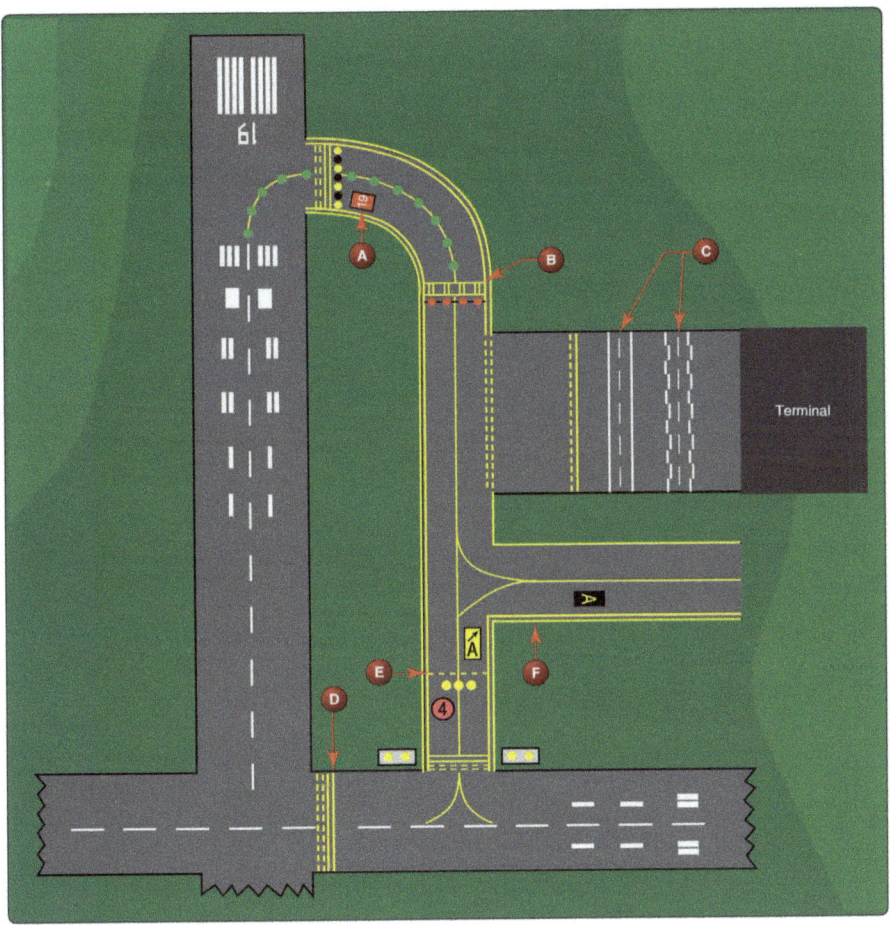

Figure 12.3. Airport Markings. (Source: FAA-CT-8080-2H, Figure 64)

Why This Matters to You

As a remote pilot operating near an airport, if you hear a pilot on the radio report that they are "holding short of runway 25," you now have a perfect mental picture of exactly where that 747 is waiting. By understanding these ground markings, you can better predict the movement of manned aircraft, which is a key part of avoiding conflict and ensuring a safe flight for everyone.

How to use this as a Remote Pilot:

- **Pick launch/landing sites** away from taxiway centerlines, hold-short points, and vehicle lanes.

- **Plan "abort" directions** that turn you away from runway/taxiway approaches or the ILS area if a manned aircraft appears.

- **Listen on CTAF** (AIM 4-1-9) at non-towered fields; the calls you hear will match what you see on the pavement, letting you predict aircraft movements.

- **Brief your VO** on these hotspots so they know exactly where to scan for traffic.

Quick Check (what the test loves)

- **Hold-short basics:** red sign + four-bar paint = **mandatory stop.**

- **ILS "ladder" marking** = keep clear when ILS is in use.

- **White ramp road stripes = vehicles**, not aircraft taxi routes.

- **Taxiway edge lines** = boundary of the movement area.

Reading the Signs: Airport Markings

Even though you won't taxi an airplane, understanding airport signs lets you predict how manned aircraft will move on the ground. Pilots use a consistent color code. Here's how to decipher it.

- Red background / white text = MANDATORY INSTRUCTION. ("Stop/hold/never enter without clearance.")

- Black background / yellow text = LOCATION. ("You are here.")

- Yellow background / black text = DIRECTION / DESTINATION. ("Go this way.")

- Black background / white numbers = RUNWAY DISTANCE REMAINING.

Figure 12.4. Runway holding position sign at takeoff end of Runway 14. (Source: FAA-H-8083-25C, Figure 14-19)

Figure 12.5. Runway safety area boundary sign. (Source: FAA-H-8083-25C, Figure 14-18)

Figure 12.6. Sea breeze and land breeze wind circulation patterns. (Source: FAA-H-8083-25C, Figure 14-22)

Figure 12.7. Sea breeze and land breeze wind circulation patterns. (Source: FAA-H-8083-25C, Figure 14-22)

What the labels A–N mean (and what you should expect)

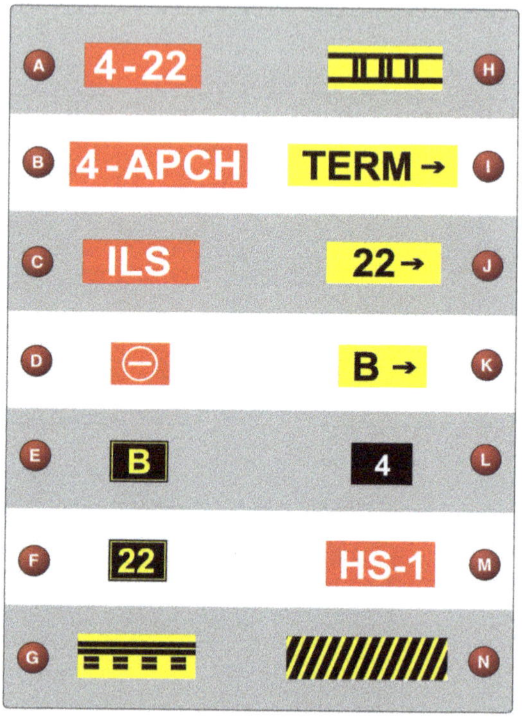

A – Runway holding position (runway designation) sign
Red "4-22". You are about to enter Runway 4/22. This is a mandatory hold point—aircraft stop here.

B – Runway approach-area hold sign
Red "4-APCH". Protects the approach end of Runway 4 when needed (e.g., low weather).

C – ILS critical-area hold sign
Red "ILS". Keeps aircraft/vehicles from disturbing the Instrument Landing System signal.

D – No-entry sign
Red circle with white bar. Area is **not** to be entered by aircraft/vehicles from this side.

E – Taxiway location sign
Black with yellow letter "B". You are **on Taxiway B.**

Figure 12.8. U.S Airport Signs. (Source: FAA-H-8083-25C, Figure 65)

F – Runway location sign
Black/yellow "22" (runway designator). You are **on Runway 22.**

G – Surface-painted direction/location aids
Yellow/black surface panels. Painted on the pavement to reinforce nearby direction/location signs where pilots can't easily see a vertical sign.

H – Runway holding position (surface symbol / companion to A)
Graphic depiction of the runway hold symbol seen at A's location.

I – Destination sign (facility)
Yellow "TERM →". Arrow to **Terminal** (or other named facility).

J – Runway direction sign
Yellow "22 →". Arrow pointing toward **Runway 22.**

K – Taxiway direction sign
Yellow "B →". Arrow to **Taxiway B.**

L – Runway distance-remaining sign
Black with white "4". **4,000 feet** of runway left (numbers are in thousands).

M – "Hot Spot" sign
Red "HS-1". Historically confusing or high-risk surface intersection.

N – Taxiway ending marker / non-movement boundary
Diagonal black/yellow stripes. The taxiway **does not continue** beyond this point (or marks a boundary to non-movement pavement).

Why this matters to Part 107 pilots

- **Predict flow:** Signs tell you where aircraft will hold, turn, and enter the runway. That lets you choose safe launch/recovery points and VO scan sectors.

- **Avoid hotspots:** Hold lines, ILS/approach holds, and **HS** areas are where aircraft bunch up–keep your drone and crew away.

- **Ramp awareness:** Yellow/black (direction) and black/yellow (location) signs on the ramp mean **vehicle and aircraft traffic**–expect jet blast/ prop wash.

Quick Exam Tips

- Red signs = **must hold/stop.**

- Black/yellow = **you are here** (taxiway/runway location).

- Yellow/black (with arrows) = **go this way** (direction/destination).

- Black/white number = thousands of feet remaining on the runway.

- **HS-# = Hot Spot**–recognize and avoid.

The Details Page: Chart Supplements

The sectional chart gives you the big picture, but what if you need to know an airport's specific operating hours, runway lengths, or CTAF frequency?

For that, you use the **Chart Supplement** (formerly called the Airport/Facility Directory). This is the official FAA booklet that contains all the detailed data for every public-use airport. The test will expect you to know that the Chart Supplement is where you find this specific information.

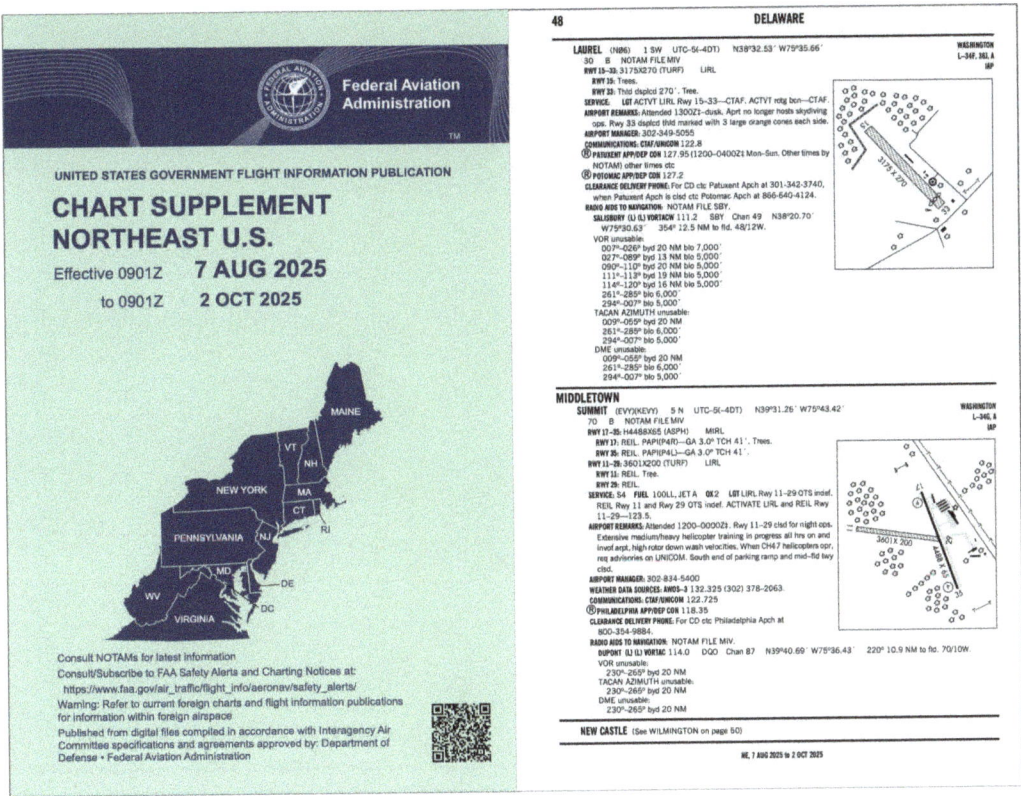

The cover of a U.S. Chart Supplement.   Page showing detailed airport information.

They are available from the FAA's Website here:
https://www.faa.gov/air_traffic/flight_info/aeronav/digital_products/dafd/

Situational Awareness is Everything

When you're flying near an airport, your situational awareness needs to be at its peak. This means knowing the answers to these questions at all times:

- Where is the airport?

- Which runways are in use? (You can often tell by listening to the radio or watching the planes).

- Where are the planes?

- Where are the helicopters? (Helicopters can fly lower and in less predictable patterns than planes).

Your Best Friends: Charts and Radios

How do you get all this information? You use the tools we've already learned about!

1. **Sectional Charts:** Your sectional chart is your map. It will show you the airport's location, its runway layout, the type of airspace it's in, and the radio frequencies you need.

2. **Notices to Air Missions (NOTAMs):** Before any flight, you must check for NOTAMs. These are time-sensitive notices about temporary changes or hazards. There are several types:

   - **NOTAM(D):** These are the most common type. They include information about runway closures, obstacles like new construction cranes, or changes in airport lighting.

   - **FDC NOTAMs:** These are regulatory in nature, such as changes to an instrument approach procedure or, most importantly for drone pilots, **Temporary Flight Restrictions (TFRs)**. A TFR is a NOTAM that defines an area where air travel is limited for a period. This can be for VIP movements (like the President), major sporting events, or natural disasters. Flying in a TFR without authorization is a serious violation.

   - **Pointer NOTAMs:** These simply point out another NOTAM, helping to highlight its importance.

     You can check for NOTAMs, including TFRs, on the FAA's website or at **1800wxbrief.com.**

3. **Aviation Radio:** This is your best tool for real-time information. Listen to the CTAF or tower frequency. You'll hear pilots announce their position and intentions, giving you a live picture of the air traffic around you. This is the single most effective thing you can do to stay safe.

Even if you're flying just outside the airport's controlled airspace, it's still a fantastic idea to monitor the local frequencies. A pilot taking off might be heading in your direction, and hearing their radio call could be the one thing that prevents a dangerous close call.

Operating near an airport is a huge responsibility, but it's also a sign that you're a trusted member of the aviation community. By being "airport savvy"–understanding the environment and using your tools–you show respect for manned aircraft pilots and prove that drones can be integrated safely into the national airspace.

Key Takeaways

1. The **traffic pattern** is the standard "highway in the sky" that manned aircraft use around an airport; know it so you can avoid it.

2. Your best tools for situational awareness near an airport are your **sectional chart** and an **aviation radio** for listening to the CTAF.

3. You must have **LAANC authorization** to fly in the controlled airspace (B, C, D, E surface) around most airports.

Likely Test Questions

1. What is the primary reason a drone pilot should be familiar with the traffic pattern at an airport?

2. What is the most effective tool for gaining real-time situational awareness when operating near an airport?

3. What are runways and taxiways?

The Practice Test

Are You Ready?

Before you sit for the real test, this chapter gives you a full-length practice exam using FAA-style questions and figures from the Airman Knowledge Testing Supplement to make sure you're ready.

Using the Airman Knowledge Testing Supplement

During the test, you'll be given a physical booklet called the **Airman Knowledge Testing Supplement**. This guide contains every chart, map, and figure you will need to answer certain questions on the exam.

While this may sound like a curveball we're throwing you at the last second—don't worry! Nearly all of the images, charts, and diagrams you've seen from the Red Raven guide have come directly from this book and are the exact same ones you will see one the test. If you've gotten this far, you are already well prepared!

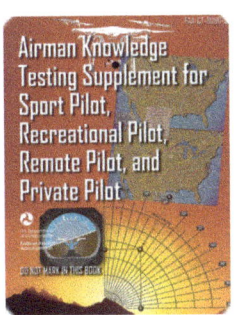

Airman Knowledge Testing Supplement

Familiarize Yourself Before the Test

While you are given the supplement at the testing center, you should not be seeing it for the first time on test day. Wasting precious minutes flipping through a 100+ page book looking for the right chart can cost you a passing grade.

The FAA makes the official testing supplement available as a **free PDF online.**

You can download the current version here: https://www.faa.gov/sites/faa.gov/files/training_testing/testing/supplements/sport_rec_private_akts.pdf

Download it and get familiar with it. Knowing the general layout—where the sectional chart legends are, where the METAR figures begin, where performance charts are located—will give you a significant advantage in speed and confidence while you're taking the test.

Do you need to read it cover-to-cover? No. The booklet serves **multiple certificates** (sport, recreational, private, and remote), so it includes more than a Part 107 pilot will be tested on. Your time is best spent getting familiar with the sections most relevant to small UAS operations.

How to Use the Supplement in the Exam

Many questions on the test are scenario-based and will direct you to a specific figure in the supplement. A question will typically begin with a phrase like, *"Refer to Figure 21..."* Your task is to turn to that figure in the booklet and use the information presented to find the correct answer.

Here are a few common examples:

- **Sectional Chart Example:** A question asks, *"Refer to Figure 22, area 2. What is the floor of the controlled airspace at the Sandpoint Airport (SZT)?"* You would flip to Figure 22 in the supplement, find the area labeled "2," locate the Sandpoint Airport, and interpret the airspace markings surrounding it to determine the answer.

- **Weather Example:** A question states, *"Refer to Figure 12. What are the current conditions for KMDW?"* You would find the list of METAR reports in Figure 12, locate the line for the station "KMDW," and decode the text to determine the wind, visibility, and cloud cover.

- **Performance Example:** A question might ask, "Refer to Figure 2. If an unmanned airplane weighs 33 pounds, what approximate weight would the airplane structure be required to support during a 30° banked turn while maintaining altitude?" You would navigate to the Load Factor chart in Figure 2, find the 30° bank angle, see it corresponds to a load factor of 1.154, and multiply that by the aircraft's weight ($33 \times 1.154 \approx 38$ lbs).

Before You Dive In – How to Use the Practice Questions

This chapter compiles a full practice test drawn from the FAA's Part 107 materials. It's designed to feel like the real thing. Many items will say *"Refer to Figure …"* and point you to the same style of charts you'll see on test day.

How to Practice (Test-Day Style)

- Time: Set a timer for 2 hours for the 60 questions (same pace as the real exam).

- Materials: Use the FAA Testing Supplement (AKTS) PDF, a calculator, scratch paper, and a pencil.

- No peeking: Treat outside sources as "off limits" while you take the practice test and don't peek at the answers. Save it to the end.

- Mark & move: If stuck after 60-90 seconds on a question, mark it and move on. Return later.

Scoring & Debrief

- Passing = 70% (aim for 42/60 or better).

- After you score, tag missed questions by trouble area (airspace, weather, charts, operations, performance, etc).

- For each missed question, open go back through this book and figure out why you answered it incorrectly.

Pro Tips

- Use the legends: If a symbol or abbreviation isn't familiar, it's in the supplement—find it fast.

- Work the figures: Sectionals (airspace floors), METAR/TAF (decode), airport signs/markings, wind/load-factor charts, Chart Supplement entries.

- Eliminate twice: Cross out two wrong answers first; choose the best remaining.

- Never leave blanks. You have a 1 in 3 chance of guessing the right answer.

When you're ready, turn the page and fly the plan.

FAA Part 107 Practice Questions

1. **What are characteristics of a moist, unstable air mass?**

   A) Turbulence and showery precipitation.
   B) Poor visibility and smooth air.
   C) Haze and smoke.

2. **According to 14 CFR part 107, how may a remote pilot operate an unmanned aircraft in Class C airspace?**

   A) The remote pilot must have prior authorization from the Air Traffic Control (ATC) facility having jurisdiction over that airspace.
   B) The remote pilot must monitor the ATC frequency from launch to recovery.
   C) The remote pilot must contact ATC after launching the unmanned aircraft.

3. **According to 14 CFR part 107, the remote pilot in command (PIC) of a small unmanned aircraft planning to operate within Class C airspace…**

   A) must use a visual observer.
   B) is required to file a flight plan.
   C) is required to receive ATC authorization.

4. **What effect does high density altitude have on the efficiency of a UA propeller?**

   A) Propeller efficiency is increased.
   B) Propeller efficiency is decreased.
   C) Density altitude does not affect propeller efficiency.

5. (Refer to FAA-CT-8080-2H, Figure 22, area 2.) At Coeur d'Alene, which frequency should be used as a Common Traffic Advisory Frequency (CTAF) to monitor airport traffic?

   A) 122.05 MHz.
   B) 135.075 MHz.
   C) 122.8 MHz.

6. Which technique should a remote pilot use to scan for traffic? A remote pilot should...

   A) systematically focus on different segments of the sky for short intervals.
   B) concentrate on relative movement detected in peripheral vision.
   C) continuously scan the sky from right to left.

7. (Refer to FAA-CT-8080-2H, Figure 2.) If an unmanned airplane weighs 33 pounds, what approximate weight would the airplane structure be required to support during a 30° banked turn while maintaining altitude?

   A) 34 pounds.
   B) 47 pounds.
   C) 38 pounds.

8. (Refer to FAA-CT-8080-2H, Figure 23, area 3.) What is the floor of the Savannah Class C airspace at the shelf area (outer circle)?

   A) 1,300 feet AGL.
   B) 1,300 feet MSL.
   C) 1,700 feet MSL.

9. (Refer to FAA-CT-8080-2H, Figure 20, area 3.) With ATC authorization, you are operating your small unmanned aircraft approximately 4 SM southeast of Elizabeth City Regional Airport (ECG). What hazard is indicated to be in that area?

   A) High density military operations in the vicinity.
   B) Unmarked balloon on a cable up to 3,008 feet AGL.
   C) Unmarked balloon on a cable up to 3,008 feet MSL.

10. (Refer to FAA-CT-8080-2H, Figure 21.) You have been hired by a farmer to inspect crops. The area to survey is in the Devil's Lake West MOA, east of area 2. How would you find out if the MOA is active?

   A) Refer to the chart legend.
   B) This information is available in the Small UAS database.
   C) Refer to the Military Operations Directory.

11. The most comprehensive information on a given airport is provided by...

   A) the Chart Supplements U.S. (formerly Airport/Facility Directory).
   B) Notices to Airmen (NOTAMs).
   C) Terminal Area Chart (TAC).

12. Identify the hazardous attitude a remote pilot displays while taking risks to impress others.

   A) Impulsivity.
   B) Invulnerability.

C) Macho.

13. (Refer to FAA-CT-8080-2H, Figure 26, area 4.) You're hired to inspect the tower under construction at 46.9°N and 98.6°W, near Jamestown Regional (JMS). What must you receive prior to flying your unmanned aircraft in this area?

A) Authorization from the military.
B) Authorization from ATC.
C) Authorization from the National Park Service.

14. (Refer to FAA-CT-8080-2H, Figure 20, area 5.) How would a remote PIC "CHECK NOTAMS" as noted in the CAUTION box regarding the unmarked balloon?

A) By using the B4UFLY mobile application.
B) By contacting the FAA district office.
C) By obtaining a briefing via an online source such as 1800WXBrief.com.

15. When adapting crew resource management (CRM) to small UA operations, CRM must be integrated into...

A) the flight portion only.
B) all phases of the operation.
C) the communications only

16. You've been hired by a TV news station to film breaking news with a small UA. You express a safety concern and the station manager tells you to "fly first, ask questions later." What hazardous attitude is this?

    A) Machismo.
    B) Invulnerability.
    C) Impulsivity.

17. A local TV station's remote pilot has had multiple near misses and two small UAS accidents. What could improve their operating safety culture?

    A) Implement a policy of no more than five crashes/incidents within 6 months.
    B) No changes are needed; some accidents are unavoidable.
    C) Recognize hazardous attitudes/situations and develop SOPs that emphasize safety.

18. (Refer to FAA-CT-8080-2H, Figure 26, area 2.) While monitoring the Cooperstown CTAF you hear an aircraft announce "midfield left downwind to RWY 13." Where is the aircraft relative to the runway?

    A) East.
    B) South.
    C) West.

19. To avoid a possible collision with a manned airplane, you estimate your small UA climbed to greater than 600 feet AGL. To whom must you report the deviation?

   A) Air Traffic Control.
   B) National Transportation Safety Board.
   C) Upon request of the FAA.

20. When operating an unmanned airplane, the remote pilot should consider that the load factor on the wings may be increased any time...

   A) the CG is shifted rearward to the aft CG limit.
   B) the airplane is subjected to maneuvers other than straight-and-level flight.
   C) the gross weight is reduced.

21. A stall occurs when the smooth airflow over the wing is disrupted and lift degenerates rapidly. This is caused when the wing...
   A) exceeds the maximum speed.
   B) exceeds maximum allowable operating weight.
   C) exceeds its critical angle of attack.

22. Safety is important prior to operating a UAS. To prevent the final "link" in the accident chain, a remote pilot must consider which methodology?
   A) Crew Resource Management.
   B) Safety Management System.
   C) Risk Management.

23. You are a remote pilot for a co-op energy service provider. After a 15-hour drive to a remote area, fatigue impacts your abilities. Fatigue can be recognized...

   A) easily by an experienced pilot.
   B) as being in an impaired state.
   C) by an ability to overcome sleep deprivation.

24. (Refer to FAA-CT-8080-2H, Figure 21.) What airport is located approximately 47°40' N latitude and 101°26' W longitude?

   A) Mercer County Regional Airport.
   B) Semshenko Airport.
   C) Garrison Airport.

25. (Refer to FAA-CT-8080-2H, Figure 12.) What are the current conditions for Chicago Midway Airport (KMDW)?

   A) Sky 700 feet overcast, visibility 1-1/2 SM, rain.
   B) Sky 7,000 feet overcast, visibility 1-1/2 SM, heavy rain.
   C) Sky 700 feet overcast, visibility 11, occasionally 2 SM, with rain.

26. (Refer to FAA-CT-8080-2H, Figure 12.) The wind direction and velocity at KJFK is from...

   A) 180° true at 4 knots.
   B) 180° magnetic at 4 knots.
   C) 040° true at 18 knots.

27.According to 14 CFR part 107, what is required to operate a small UA within 30 minutes after official sunset?

A) Use of anti-collision lights.
B) Must be operated in a rural area.
C) Use of a transponder.

28.To ensure the unmanned aircraft center of gravity (CG) limits are not exceeded, follow the aircraft loading instructions specified in the...

A) Pilot's Operating Handbook (POH) or UAS Flight Manual.
B) Aeronautical Information Manual (AIM).
C) Aircraft Weight and Balance Handbook.

29.According to 14 CFR part 107, who is responsible for determining the performance of a small unmanned aircraft?

A) Remote pilot in command.
B) Manufacturer.
C) Owner or operator.

30.(Refer to FAA-CT-8080-2H, Figure 59, area 2.) The chart shows a gray line with "VR1667, VR1617, VR1638, and VR1668." Could this area present a hazard to small UA operations?

A) No, all operations will be above 400 feet.
B) Yes, this is a Military Training Route from the surface to 1,500 feet AGL.
C) Yes, the defined route provides traffic separation to manned aircraft.

31.(Refer to FAA-CT-8080-2H, Figure 26.) What does the line of latitude at area 4 measure?

A) The degrees of latitude east and west of the Prime Meridian.
B) The degrees of latitude north and south of the equator.
C) The degrees of latitude east and west of the line that passes through Greenwich, England.

32.Under what condition should the operator of a small UA establish scheduled maintenance protocol?

A) When the manufacturer does not provide a maintenance schedule.
B) UAS does not need a required maintenance schedule.
C) When the FAA requires you to, following an accident.

33.According to 14 CFR part 107, the responsibility to inspect the small UAS to ensure it is in a safe operating condition rests with the...

A) remote pilot in command.
B) visual observer.
C) owner of the small UAS.

34.According to 14 CFR part 48, when would a small UA owner not be permitted to register it?

A) If the owner is less than 13 years of age.
B) All persons must register their small UA.
C) If the owner does not have a valid U.S. driver's license.

35. **According to 14 CFR part 48, when must a person register a small UA with the FAA?**

    A) All civilian small UAs weighing greater than 0.55 pounds must be registered regardless of intended use.
    B) When the small UA is used for any purpose other than as a model aircraft.
    C) Only when the operator will be paid for commercial services.

36. **Which is true regarding the presence of alcohol within the human body?**

    A) A small amount of alcohol increases vision acuity.
    B) Consuming an equal amount of water will increase the destruction of alcohol and alleviate a hangover.
    C) Judgment and decision-making can be adversely affected by even small amounts of alcohol.

37. **When using a small UA in a commercial operation, who is responsible for briefing participants about emergency procedures?**

    A) The FAA inspector-in-charge.
    B) The lead visual observer.
    C) The remote PIC.

38. **What are the characteristics of stable air?**

    A) Good visibility and steady precipitation.
    B) Poor visibility and steady precipitation.
    C) Poor visibility and intermittent precipitation.

39. You received an outlook briefing via 1800wxbrief.com indicating a low-level temperature inversion with high relative humidity. What weather would you expect?

A) Smooth air, poor visibility, fog, haze, or low clouds.
B) Light wind shear, poor visibility, haze, and light rain.
C) Turbulent air, poor visibility, fog, low stratus clouds, and showery precipitation.

40. When may a remote pilot reduce the intensity of an aircraft's lights during a night flight?

A) Never.
B) When a manned aircraft is in the vicinity of the sUAS.
C) When it is in the interest of safety to dim the lights.

41. What must a person manipulating the controls do if standard Remote ID fails during a flight?

A) Land the aircraft as soon as practicable.
B) Notify the nearest FAA Air Traffic facility.
C) Activate the aircraft's navigation lights.

42. Where must a small unmanned aircraft's serial number be listed when using either standard Remote ID or a broadcast module?

A) The aircraft's Document of Compliance.
B) The manufacturer's Method of Compliance.
C) The Certificate of Aircraft Registration.

43. **When preparing for a night flight, what should an sUAS pilot be aware of after assembling/conducting a preflight using a bright flashlight or work light?**

    A) Once adapted to darkness, eyes are relatively immune to bright lights.
    B) It takes approximately 30 minutes for eyes to fully adapt to darkness.
    C) Use a flashlight equipped with LED lights to facilitate night vision.

44. **To conduct Category 1 operations, a remote PIC must use a small unmanned aircraft that weighs...**

    A) 0.55 pounds or less.
    B) 0.65 pounds or less.
    C) 0.75 pounds or less.

45. **Which Category of small unmanned aircraft must have an airworthiness certificate issued by the FAA?**

    A) 4.
    B) 3.
    C) 2.

46. Your surveying company sponsors a race team at the Indianapolis 500. A TFR has been issued over the race area you plan to fly. In this situation…

    A) you may fly your drone in the TFR since your company is sponsoring a team.
    B) the TFR applies to all aircraft; you may not fly in the area without a Certificate of Waiver or Authorization.
    C) flying your drone is allowed if you notify all non-participating people of the closed-course UA operation.

47. Under Part 107, what is the maximum groundspeed for a small unmanned aircraft?

    A) 87 knots (100 mph).
    B) 100 knots (115 mph).
    C) 100 mph indicated airspeed.

48. You're inspecting a 250-ft AGL tower on flat terrain. While remaining within 400 ft horizontally of the structure, what is your maximum allowed altitude?

    A) 400 ft AGL.
    B) 650 ft AGL.
    C) 1,000 ft AGL.

49. What are the minimum weather requirements for sUAS operations under Part 107?

    A) 3 SM visibility; 500 ft below clouds and 2,000 ft horizontal from clouds.
    B) 1 SM visibility; clear of clouds.

C) 5 SM visibility; 1,000 ft above and 2,000 ft horizontal from clouds.

50. **When should a remote pilot use the FAA DroneZone instead of LAANC for airspace authorization?**

A) When LAANC isn't available or you need altitude above the published grid.
B) For all Class G operations.
C) To file NOTAMs for UAS flights.

51. **Which operation is exempt from broadcasting Remote ID?**

A) Flying inside a FRIA (FAA-Recognized Identification Area).
B) Any flight with a drone weighing under 0.55 lb, regardless of use.
C) Any flight in Class G airspace.

52. **Under Part 107, an accident must be reported to the FAA within 10 days when it results in...**

A) Any damage to the UA or accessories.
B) Serious injury or loss of consciousness, or property damage > $500 (not including the UA).
C) Any flight termination or return-to-home event.

53. **When using a Visual Observer (VO) to help meet VLOS, what is required?**

A) VO must have binoculars.
B) Continuous, immediate communication with the RPIC so see-and-avoid duties are met.
C) VO must be within 50 feet of the RPIC.

54. **Right-of-way: A small unmanned aircraft must yield to...**

A) Only powered airplanes and helicopters.
B) Only balloons and gliders.
C) All other aircraft.

55. **Operating from a moving vehicle under Part 107 is permitted when...**

A) Over a sparsely populated area and not transporting another person's property for compensation or hire.
B) You are in Class G airspace.
C) You file a NOTAM.

56. **You begin to feel tingling and lightheaded during flight—classic signs of hyperventilation. What should you do?**

A) Breathe faster to increase oxygen.
B) Slow your breathing rate and talk aloud to regulate CO_2/O_2 balance.
C) Immediately switch to ATC oxygen.

57. **On a sectional, a dashed magenta circle around an airport indicates...**

A) Class D surface area.
B) Class C shelf area.
C) Class E surface area (to the surface).

58. **Which CTAF phrase is discouraged by the AIM at non-towered airports?**

    A) "Anysville traffic, Skyhawk 123AB, left downwind Runway One-Eight, Anysville."
    B) "Any traffic in the area, please advise."
    C) "Smith Field traffic, Red Raven unmanned aircraft, two miles east at or below 400 feet, Smith Field."

59. **In a METAR, BKN020 indicates...**

    A) Broken clouds at 2,000 ft AGL (ceiling).
    B) Broken clouds at 20,000 ft AGL.
    C) Few clouds at 2,000 ft AGL.

60. **Which alcohol rule reflects Part 107 requirements?**

    A) No BAC limit applies if you're outdoors.
    B) You may fly within 4 hours of drinking if BAC < 0.04%.
    C) No flying within 8 hours of alcohol consumption, no BAC ≥ 0.04%, and no impairment.

Answer Key

1. A	16.C	31.B	46.B
2. A	17.C	32.A	47.A
3. C	18.A	33.A	48.B
4. B	19.A	34.A	49.A
5. C	20.B	35.A	50.A
6. A	21.C	36.C	51.A
7. C	22.C	37.C	52.B
8. B	23.B	38.B	53.B
9. C	24.C	39.A	54.C
10.A	25.A	40.C	55.A
11.A	26.A	41.A	56.B
12.C	27.A	42.A	57.C
13.B	28.A	43.B	58.B
14.C	29.A	44.A	59.A
15.B	30.B	45.A	60.C

How Did You Do?

Great work completing the practice exam! Now, it's time to tally up your score.

Are You Ready for the Real Exam?

We've found that students who score 50 or more correct answers (an 83% or higher) are in a great position to pass the official FAA exam. If this is you, congratulations! Your hard work is paying off.

Need More Review?

If you scored lower than 50, don't worry—this is exactly what practice tests are for. This is a perfect opportunity to pinpoint your weak spots. Go back through each question you missed and identify the topic. Was it airspace, weather, or specific regulations? Revisit those sections in the guide to strengthen your understanding.

When you feel you have a stronger grasp on the material, take this practice test again. The goal is to see progress and build confidence.

Ready to Schedule Your Test?

If you're feeling confident with the questions and your score reflects that, it's time to get your test on the books. Let's move on to the next chapter, where we'll walk you through the entire process of scheduling your Part 107 exam.

Scheduling Your Test

Obtaining Your FAA Tracking Number & Scheduling Your Test

PSI Services handles the administration of FAA examinations through approximately800 testing facilities nationwide.

Your examination is officially titled the Unmanned Aircraft General-Small (UAG).

Tests are available continuously throughout the year, allowing you to schedule based on your readiness.

Two-Phase Registration Process

Phase 1: Establish Your IACRA Account

Navigate to the FAA's IACRA portal **https://iacra.faa.gov/IACRA/** and follow these steps:

1. Select "Register" (located in the upper right section)

2. Choose "Applicant" from the available options

3. Bypass the "Certificate Information" area entirely

4. Complete the remaining required fields

Upon completion, you'll receive your FAA Tracking Number (FTN) - this is essential for proceeding.

Phase 2: Schedule Through PSI

With your FTN secured, create your PSI account.

Navigate to the PSI's website **https://faa.psiexams.com/faa/login** and follow these steps:

1. Select "Create an Account" (located in the middle of the page)

2. Complete the remaining required fields

3. After account creation, sign in and choose 'Select'

4. Type 'UAG' into the search field

5. Pick 'Unmanned Aircraft Systems' from the available choices

6. Click 'Select' to continue

Important Scheduling Details

Two fields often cause confusion during booking:

1. **Authorization Category:** Unlike traditional pilot certifications, drone pilot candidates don't require instructor endorsements or authorization documents. Simply select 'None' for this field.

2. **Number of Attempts:** First-time test takers: Enter '1'. If you're retaking the exam: Enter '2', '3', etc., based on your previous attempts.

This straightforward process ensures you're properly registered for your Remote Pilot certification exam. Once you've completed both phases, you'll be all set with your test appointment!

Test Day Preparation

Test Day Preparation Guide

This guide covers essential items to bring to your testing facility and valuable strategies for test success. Students consistently report these recommendations as particularly beneficial, so please review this information thoroughly.

Arrival Time

Plan to arrive at least 20-30 minutes before your scheduled time. The check-in process includes identity verification and system registration, which often takes longer than expected. Factor this extra time into your travel schedule and anticipate that staff may work through procedures slowly.

Required Identification Documents

In order to take the exam, you'll need to bring a valid form of identification with you that shows a photo, date of birth, signature, and physical residential address. US citizens and resident aliens require one form of ID while Non-US Citizens require two.

US Citizens and Resident Aliens need to bring:

- **Current photo identification with signature** that can include one of the following:
    - Driver permit or license (issued by a US state or territory)
    - US Government identification card
    - US military identification card
    - Passport
    - Alien residency card

Non-US Citizens need to bring:

1. **Valid passport** PLUS a
2. **Current identification card** that can include one of the following:
    - Driver permit or license (issued by a US state or territory) or
    - Identification card issued by any government entity

Test Format and Structure

You'll complete the exam at a computer workstation within a two-hour time limit.

Key test details:

1. **Format:** Multiple-choice questions only

2. **Total questions:** 60 (occasionally 63 if pilot questions are included; only 60 count toward your score)

3. **Answer options:** Three choices per question (A, B, C)

4. **Question independence:** Each question stands alone; answers don't affect other questions

5. **Visual elements:** Some questions include chart or map references

6. **Passing requirement:** 70% minimum (42 correct answers needed)

7. **Time allowance:** Two hours maximum

Here's how the FAA breaks down what percentage of the exam are on which topics.

TOPIC	PERCENT OF EXAM
Operations	35-40%
Regulations	15-25%
Airspace	15-25%
Weather	11-16%
Performance	7-11%

Knowledge area distribution varies, though students frequently report Sectional Chart questions comprising 30-40% of their exam, despite official guidelines showing different percentages.

Recommended Equipment

Many test-takers report difficulty reading Sectional Charts during the exam. Common issues include inadequate room lighting, vision challenges, or the inherently small print on these charts. A magnifying glass is permitted and highly recommended to help identify chart symbols clearly.

Permitted Items

Testing centers allow very limited items:

1. Magnifying glass

2. Basic calculator (for Load Factor calculations)

* All electronic devices, including phones, must be surrendered before testing

Testing centers provide:

1. Paper

2. Writing instruments

3. Printed Test Supplement

4. Computer-based calculator available on-screen

Strategic Test Approach

Before your actual exam begins, you'll complete a practice tutorial. This familiarizes you with navigation features including answer selection, question flagging, time tracking, and software functions. Complete this tutorial thoroughly rather than rushing through.

Effective testing strategies:

1. Remember only one answer is fully correct; other options contain partial information, errors, or common misconceptions

2. Flag challenging questions for later review; complete easier items first

3. When uncertain, select the most conservative option

4. Reference the Sectional Chart legend in your Test Supplement (located after the Table of Contents) for chart-related questions

5. Attempt every question since incorrect answers don't reduce your score.

What Happens Immediately After the Test?

The moment you click the final "Submit" button on your exam, your results are calculated and will appear on the screen instantly. You'll know right away whether you passed. Before you leave, the testing center proctor will print out your official **Airman Knowledge Test Report (AKTR)**. This is the most important document you will receive that day. **Do not leave without it.**

Your AKTR will show three key pieces of information:

1. **Your final score** (e.g., 92%).

2. **Your unique 17-digit Knowledge Test ID**, which is essential for your official application.

3. **Learning statement codes** for any questions you missed, which can help you review your weak areas.

Once you have this official, printed report in hand, your work at the testing center is done, and you are free to leave. The next step is to use that report to apply for your certificate. We'll discuss that next.

Post Test Procedures

You Passed! Now Get Your Certificate pilot certificate

Congratulations on passing the FAA Aeronautical Knowledge Test! That's a huge accomplishment.

Passing the exam is the first major step, but it doesn't automatically issue your certificate. You now need to complete a formal application through the FAA's online portal. This process triggers a required Transportation Security Administration (TSA) background check to verify your eligibility for a Remote Pilot Certificate.

Your testing center should provide you with instructions, but this guide will walk you through the entire process from start to finish.

Before You Begin: A Quick Checklist

To make the application process as smooth as possible, have these items ready:

- **A Recommended Browser:** The FAA's IACRA system works best with Google Chrome or Mozilla Firefox. Be sure to enable pop-ups in your browser settings.

- **Your Test Report:** Have your official Airman Knowledge Test Report (AKTR) handy. You will need the 17-digit Knowledge Test ID from this document.

- **Matching Legal Name:** Double-check that the legal name you use for the application exactly matches the government-issued photo ID you used at the testing center.

Step-by-Step IACRA Application

Navigate to the FAA's IACRA portal: **https://iacra.faa.gov/**

1. **Log In and Start New Application.** Log in with your FAA Tracking Number (FTN) and password. From your applicant dashboard, select "Start New Application" and choose Pilot as the application type. Under Certifications, select Remote Pilot - Initial.

2. **Complete Your Information.** Fill out the Personal Information and Supplementary Data sections. Most of this information should auto-populate from your account registration. Review it for accuracy and save your progress.

3. **Enter Your Knowledge Test ID.** In the "Basis of Issuance" section, you must enter the Knowledge Test ID found on your AKTR. Keep a copy of this report for your records.

   Important Note: It can take up to 48 hours for your test results to appear in the IACRA system after you complete the exam. If the system can't find your ID, wait a day and try again.

4. **Review and Sign Electronically.** The final step is to review your entire application summary for accuracy. You will be required to view three documents (the Pilots' Bill of Rights, the Privacy Act statement, and the application review) before signing. Once you've reviewed everything, you will sign and submit the application electronically.

What Happens Next?

- **TSA Vetting:** Once submitted, your application is automatically sent for a required Transportation Security Administration (TSA) security background check. This entire process is 100% online, and you do not need to do anything further (like visit an office or provide fingerprints). The timing can vary, but the check is typically completed within a few days to a few weeks. Your only responsibility is to ensure the information on your IACRA application was accurate.

- **Temporary Certificate:** After the TSA background check is complete, you will receive an email notification that your temporary certificate is ready. Processing times vary, so keep an eye on your inbox. You can then log back into IACRA to download and print this temporary certificate. This is your legal authorization to conduct Part 107 operations, and you must have it with you (in physical or digital form) during flights.

- **Permanent Certificate:** Your permanent plastic certificate card will typically arrive by mail within 6-8 weeks after your temporary certificate is issued.

Staying Current and Legal

Congratulations

You've passed your test and you have your Remote Pilot Certificate! So, you're set for life, right? Not quite. Just like licensed drivers have to renew their licenses, drone pilots need to stay up-to-date on the latest rules and procedures. This is done through a process called recurrent training.

Your Part 107 Remote Pilot Certificate is valid for 24 calendar months. This means if you passed your test on August 10, 2026, your privileges would be valid until the end of August 2028. To continue flying commercially after that date, you must complete recurrent training and the associated test.

Renewing You Certificate: The Recurrent Training Process

Wait?! There's more training? And more testing? Well, yes. Don't worry, the hard part is over.

To keep your certificate active, the FAA requires pilots to complete a recurrent training course. Fortunately, this process is much simpler than the initial exam. You don't have to go back to a testing center or pay another fee.

The FAA provides the required training for free on its FAA Safety Team (FAASafety.gov) website. The official course is called **"Part 107 Small UAS Recurrent (ALC-677),"** and it's a self-paced, online module you can complete from home. It is designed to be a straightforward educational review that ensures you remain a safe and compliant pilot.

Here's what makes the process manageable:

- **Open-Book Exam:** The final exam for the recurrent training is open book. You are allowed and encouraged to use the course materials and any other official FAA resources to find the correct answers. The goal is to ensure you understand the material, not to test your memory under pressure.

- **Unlimited Attempts:** You must achieve a score of 100% to pass the exam and receive your completion certificate. However, you can take the test as many times as you like. If you don't pass on the first try, you can review the questions you missed and retake it until you get a perfect score.

- **Time Commitment:** The training is self-paced. Most pilots report that it takes approximately 1 to 2 hours to complete the entire course, including the learning modules and the final exam.

How to Complete Your Recurrent Training

Here's what you'll need to do:

1. **Go to https://www.faasafety.gov:** Create an account or log in to the FAA Safety Team website.

2. **Find the Course:** Search for the course by its official name, "Part 107 Small UAS Recurrent," or by its course code, **ALC-677**.

3. **Complete the Training:** Go through the training modules. The course will review key concepts and teach you about any new rules that have been implemented since your last test.

4. **Take the Exam:** At the end of the course, there is an online, open-book exam. You must get **100%** of the questions correct, but you can retake it as many times as you need to.

5. **Save Your Certificate:** Once you pass, you will receive a certificate of completion. You must save a digital or physical copy of this certificate. You are required to present it along with your original Part 107 certificate upon request by the FAA or law enforcement.

Final Thoughts

Your Flight Path as a Remote Pilot

You've made it! From learning the difference between Class B and Class G airspace to passing your exam and now understanding how to maintain your certificate, you've completed the foundational step of your aviation journey. This guide was designed to give you the knowledge to pass the test, but the true learning begins now, every time you fly.

Your Remote Pilot Certificate is more than just a license; it's a commitment to safety and professionalism. The skies are a shared space, and as a certificated pilot, you are a steward of that space. Continue to practice good aeronautical decision-making, stay informed about new technology and regulations, and always make safety the final authority on any flight.

The world of unmanned aviation is full of incredible opportunities. We wish you the best of luck as you take to the skies, whether you're capturing stunning aerial photos, surveying land, or innovating in ways we haven't even imagined yet. Congratulations on your achievement!

Fly safe.

Continue Your Journey

Passing the FAA Part 107 exam is only the first step. The real mission begins now – every flight is an opportunity to sharpen your skills, expand your knowledge, and grow as a professional remote pilot.

At **Red Raven UAS**, we're here to support you beyond the test. Explore our online resources, advanced training programs, and real-world insights designed to help you fly safer, smarter, and with confidence.

Continue your journey at **https://redravenuas.com**

About the Authors

Michael Wilson's expertise lies in making the complex simple and the technical understandable. As a writer and director for television, advertising, and educational media, his job has always been to make sophisticated topics engaging for a wide audience. He brings this passion to the drone world, drawing on his experience as a former Director at DJI, where he helped shape how the industry's leading technology is communicated to pilots and the public.

Derrick Ward is a nationally recognized public safety aviation expert with 35 years of service in the Los Angeles City Fire Department. In this role, he was instrumental in building one of the nation's largest and most respected public safety drone programs. Derrick has trained hundreds of first responders and commercial pilots to operate drones in the most demanding environments, from active wildfires and HAZMAT incidents to search-and-rescue missions. He is a private pilot, a Certified Fire Instructor, and holds a Part 107 Remote Pilot Certificate.

Together, Michael and Derrick founded Red Raven UAS with a shared mission: to cut through the dense jargon of aviation and provide clear, practical training that prepares pilots for both the FAA exam and the challenges of real-world flying.

Notes

Notes